Day by Day

Day by Day

with Celestine Sibley

DOUBLEDAY & COMPANY, INC.

GARDEN CITY, NEW YORK

1975

Library of Congress Cataloging in Publication Data

Sibley, Celestine
    Day by day with Celestine Sibley

    1. Quotations, English. I. Title.
    PN6075.S5   828'.02
    ISBN 0-385-11108-8
    Library of Congress Catalog Card Number 75-7257

Grateful acknowledgment is made to the following for permission to reprint previously published material:

Oxford University Press, Inc.: excerpt from "The House of Dust" in *Collected Poems* by Conrad Aiken. Copyright 1953 by Conrad Aiken. Dodd, Mead & Company: excerpt from *The Golden Book of Prayer* by Donald B. Aldrich. The Viking Press, Inc.: excerpt from *My Lord What a Morning* by Marian Anderson. Copyright © 1956 by Marian Anderson. Macmillan Publishing Co., Inc.: excerpt from *The Dollmaker* by Harriette Simpson Arnow. Copyright 1954 by Harriette Simpson Arnow; excerpt from the poem "We thank Thee for the joy of common things" in *Riders at the Gate* by Joseph Auslander. Copyright 1938 by Joseph Auslander, renewed 1966 by Louis and Anna Mary Auslander. University of Missouri Press and the author: excerpt from *The Three Worlds of Man* by Stringfellow Barr. Copyright © 1963 by The Curators of the University of Missouri. Published by Graphicopy Inc.: excerpts from *Wino's, Dino's & Dingbats* by Wilson A. Barkman. Farrar, Straus and Giroux, Inc.: excerpt from *What the Jews Believe* by Philip Bernstein. Copyright 1950 by Philip S. Bernstein. Harold Matson Company, Inc.: excerpt from "A Medicine for Melancholy" by Ray Bradbury. Copyright © 1959 by Ray Bradbury. Published by World Publishing Company: excerpts from *Wake Up and Live* by Dorothea Brande. Marel Brown: excerpt from *Fence Corners*. Random House, Inc.: excerpt from *The Grass Harp* by Truman Capote. Copyright 1952 by Truman Capote. Hawthorn Books, Inc.: excerpt from *Reflections on Life* by Dr. Alexis Carrel. A. P. Watt & Sons/Miss D. E. Collins: excerpt from *All Is Grist* by G. K. Chesterton. Houghton Mifflin Company: excerpts from *The Hinge of Fate, IV* by Winston S. Churchill. Copyright 1950 by Houghton Mifflin Company. Paul R. Reynolds, Inc.: excerpt from *A Prophet in His Own Country*, edited by Kenneth S. Davis. Published by Cokesbury Press: excerpts from *Wit & Wisdom of Warren Akin Candler*, edited by E. F. Dempsey. Harper & Row, Publishers, Inc.: excerpt from *Three Paths of God and Man* by Rabbi Samuel H. Dresner. Copyright © 1960 by Samuel H. Dresner. Simon & Schuster,

To Isabelle Taylor and Larry Ashmead

Day by Day

From one with a lifelong aversion to reading directions on all cans and cartons, one who has worn out many a household appliance without once glancing at the how-to fine print that came with it, this may seem the ultimate presumption—a book that proposes to offer directions and how-to suggestions for living.

How dare you, unless you can hold up your own life as a model of rectitude, achievement, and halcyon happiness, open your mouth about the stubborn secrets of living?

Cooter, a black friend of my childhood, received advice by testing the adviser: "Is you tried it yourself? Don't gimme no *maybe's!*"

"Maybe's" are all that many of us are ever sure of. We stumble along, fumbling for answers, questioning, seeking, sometimes angry and rebellious, more often clumsily hurting and embarrassingly vulnerable and sometimes knowing a happiness that runs all the way from contentment to ecstasy.

As an only child living in the country, I early found companionship in reading—anything that came to hand. Sometimes a not very good poet sounded an idea that to my naïve mind sparked and rang with fresh and urgent truth. I remember an Ella Wheeler Wilcox poem that told me for the first time:

"Each sorrow has its meaning
By the sorrowing oft unguessed . . ."

I believed it and was comforted by it and I guess I still am. Unfortunately, she went on to say in the same poem something I have to question: "Whatever is, is best." Where would the world be if we could accept such claptrap as that?

Along the way there have been many others, some better than Ella Wheeler Wilcox and possibly some worse, who have cheered and comforted me, sometimes pushing me toward fresh endeavor, sometimes making me want to be better and kinder, more often than not just saying in effect, "Buck up, old girl. It's not as bad as you think."

Since we are all so greatly influenced by what we read, I could have wished that, like the Georgia mountain poet, Byron Herbert Reece, who knew only the Bible and Shakespeare in his childhood, I had been nurtured by the luminous words and thoughts of the best scholars. Instead, where I grew up all sorts of trash was available. I read *Elsie Dinsmore* and, for a time, gave up going to movies on Sunday. I read Bernarr MacFadden's *Physical Culture* and took to swimming in the millpond in wintertime. I read *The Deerslayer* and to this day am hooked on the notion that I have to point my toes straight ahead, Indian-fashion, when I walk.

But, happily, if you read enough you are bound to read something good. A high school English teacher, Miss Lura Moore, was trying to snag our wandering minds with Wordsworth's "The World Is Too Much with Us" when I discovered, by jumping ahead in Literature & Life Book

IV, Edna St. Vincent Millay's "O World I Cannot Hold Thee Close Enough."

Its impact on me was almost as physical as the hurricane winds of September or a dam-breaking flood in April. She wrote what I knew about. What could the preachy Wordsworth, moralizing about the world's "getting and spending," say to a depression-era child who thought money was about as real and available as the Golden Fleece? Sure, if you could get it, you spent it—but who ever had it? Millay's poetry hurt my flesh and sang in my head and made me look again at what was all around me—"woods that all but ache and sag with color." I turned my back on the ancients and took to modern poetry with a vengeance, even embracing, heaven help me, Edgar A. Guest somewhere along the line. (I still think he was marvelously astute to know that it "takes a heap o' livin' in a house t'make it home.")

It wasn't until I was grown up and married that I returned to elder writers and then it wasn't by choice. My husband brought to our marriage, as an embarrassing evidence of his teen-age folly, the *Harvard Classics*. He had had his first job and a girl and he hadn't wanted Dr. Eliot's Five-Foot Shelf, but by the time the salesman got through with him, he later confessed, the salesman had to fight to keep him from buying the deluxe edition in vellum binding.

I didn't want those gloomy-looking black books. They looked neither bright nor readable and they didn't do anything to zip up the décor of our living room. Besides, I thought *sets* of books were tacky. But I came to read around in them, not thoroughly, not deeply (I'm certain

Dr. Eliot intended some of them for doorstops!), but often with pleasure.

Whatever erudition Dr. Eliot hoped to bring to American households I missed. (I was too eager to drop Pascal and Kant the minute *The Saturday Evening Post* arrived with the latest installment of a Charlotte Armstrong mystery.) But I met Plato and Epictetus and "the last and the loftiest" of the pagan moralists, Marcus Aurelius. I discovered Emerson and Thoreau and even looked in again on Wordsworth—a happy reader who found many of her needs answered in the printed words of better and brighter minds.

I don't believe, as Mr. Emerson has it, that what is true for me in my own heart is true for all men. But on the off-chance that what has been helpful to me might be helpful or pleasurable to others, I offer—a day at a time—what Shakespeare called an "alms-basket of words" filched from a lifelong feast.

JANUARY 1

This is the day which the Lord hath made; we will rejoice and be glad in it.   Psalm 118:24

JANUARY 2

Begin. To begin is half the work.   Ausonius

Nowhere is this so effective a cudgel as in the field of writing. It's the starting, moving, getting under way that frees us from the grip of inaction and procrastination. If it applies to work, why not to any hoped for change or improvement?

JANUARY 3

If you have known how to compose your life, you have accomplished a great deal more than the man who knows how to compose a book. Have you been able to take your stride? You have done more than the man who has taken cities and empires. The great and glorious masterpiece of man is to live to the point. All other things—to reign, to hoard, to build—are at most but inconsiderate props and appendages.
                                                        Montaigne

Today's young people speak often of "finding" themselves, as if they were lost balls or mislaid gloves. They have a lot on their side. Maybe the rest of us haven't dared to take time out and examine our lives, to "compose" them, as the sixteenth-century Frenchman suggests. Emerson is with the young: "Why should we have only two or three ways of life and not thousands?"

JANUARY 4

Life is short and we have not too much time for gladdening the hearts of those who are traveling the dark way with us. Oh, be swift to love! Make haste to be kind!
                                                        Henri F. Amiel

JANUARY 5

A man is relieved and gay when he has put his heart into his work and done his best; but what he has said or done otherwise shall give him no peace.

Ralph Waldo Emerson

Obviously, Mr. Emerson in a day of vast leisure had the same problems that confront many of us today. He was nagged by unfinished work, had his pleasure in all else go sour because of a guilty conscience. His words in his essay on self-reliance are as modern as the nearest hippy: "Do your work, and I shall know you. Do your work, and you shall reinforce yourself."

JANUARY 6

Is it important?

A sign to be posted wherever the eye first falls in time of worry and self-pity. Is the current fear or hurt of sufficient magnitude to deserve such attention? Or should you save your aching for something really important?

JANUARY 7

We have no more right to consume happiness without producing it than to consume wealth without producing it.   George Bernard Shaw

To my fundamentalist mind there's a neat and satisfying symmetry in that. It has a tit-for-tat, darkness-and-light, ebb-and-flow quality. But there really is a more generous spirit in life than that. We do get much happiness which can't be earned or deserved. The gentle rain from heaven falling on the just and unjust alike is but an example. The Bible says it with more grace and warmth than Shaw: "Freely ye have received, freely give."

JANUARY 8

Make haste to live and consider each day a life.   Seneca

JANUARY 9

Freedom is not so much a birthright as it is an achieve-
ment. We are born with freedom of choice but the way
we use our choices makes us slaves or free men. Inner
freedom of this kind is the last thing a man attains and it
is what St. Paul calls the "glorious liberty of the children
of God."   Bishop Fulton J. Sheen

JANUARY 10

Do not wish to be anything but what you are and try to
be that perfectly.   St. Francis de Sales

Perfection is an odd, old-fashioned word. Who seeks it
any more? Make do, get by, do what you have to do pass-
ably well—these are more in the tenor of the times. And
then you see and are shamed by a perfectionist—the
court-appointed lawyer impassionedly defending his client
with no thought of fee, the garage mechanic who knows
what he is about under the hood of your car and per-
forms with skill and precision, the cook who works with
love and imagination. Walt Whitman wrote that in the

"measureless grossness of the slag" of the earth there nestles, enclosed and safe within its central heart, a seed of perfection. Could the same be true of people? It's worth looking for and nurturing.

JANUARY 11

To have faith requires courage, the ability to take a risk, the readiness even to accept pain and disappointment. Whoever insists on safety and security as primary conditions of life cannot have faith; whoever shuts himself off in a system of defense, where distance and possession are his means of security, makes himself a prisoner. To be loved, and to love, need courage, the courage to judge certain values as the ultimate concern—and to take the jump and stake everything on these values.

Erich Fromm

JANUARY 12

O God, please make me easy to live with.

Artist Carolyn Becknell Mann saw that sign posted in the sanctuary of a Negro church in downtown Atlanta and was so charmed with it she asked permission to copy it and have it reproduced to give her friends. To those of us who own one of the delightfully embellished little signs it is a quick and cheerful warning against what Dr. Henry Drummond called "the sins of the disposition."

JANUARY 13

The peculiarity of ill temper is that it is the vice of the virtuous.   Dr. Henry Drummond

The Scottish minister, who lived from 1851 to 1897 and wrote the beloved and enduring book *The Greatest Thing in the World,* was the first person I ever found to condemn the Prodigal Son's righteous, stay-at-home brother as a "dark and loveless soul." "Look at the Elder Brother," he directs, "moral, hard-working, patient, dutiful . . . look at this man, this baby, sulking outside his own father's door. 'He was angry,' we read, 'and would not go in.' Look at the effect upon the father, upon the servants, upon the happiness of the guests. Judge of the effect upon the Prodigal—and how many prodigals are kept out of the Kingdom of God by the unlovely character of those who profess to be inside?"

The infirmities of the elder brother's nature include jealousy, anger, pride, uncharity, cruelty, self-right-

eousness, touchiness, doggedness, and sullenness, said Dr.
Drummond—all "sins against Love and a hundred times
more base" than sins of the body.

JANUARY 14

*The load of tomorrow, added to that of yesterday,
carried today, makes the strongest falter. We must learn
to shut out the future as tightly as the past.*

Sir William Osler

JANUARY 15

*There is nothing more notable in Socrates than that he
found time, when he was an old man, to learn music and
dancing and thought it well spent.* Montaigne

JANUARY 16

*The jealous are troublesome to others but a torment to
themselves. Jealousy is a kind of civil war in the soul,
where judgement and imagination are at perpetual jars.*

This civil dissension in the mind, like that of the body politick, commits great disorders and lays all waste.
William Penn

JANUARY 17

The law of nature is: Do the thing and you shall have the power; but they who do not do the thing have not the power.
Dorothea Brande

The author of *Wake Up and Live,* a best seller of the 1930s, believed that the reason we do not accomplish the things we profess to want to do is that there is built into us a will to fail. Sometimes we are unconscious of it. Sometimes we enjoy failure's compensations. All that is necessary to break the spell of inertia and frustration, said she, is to: Act as if it were impossible to fail. And if you are not kidding and want to do something—travel, write, learn a language, build a house, anything—do something toward it every day.

JANUARY 18

Little children, love one another.   Father James Keller

Father Keller, founder of The Christophers, tells a moving story about how John the Evangelist, when he was an old man, feeble and senile, came to bore his friends by repeating himself wherever he spoke. He always said, "Little children, love one another." Finally wearying of the same admonition, the disciples asked him why he didn't change his tune. It was, said the old man, a command of the Lord: "Do this alone and it is enough."

JANUARY 19

I need not tell you that true patriotism sometimes requires of men to act contrary at one period to that which it does at another, and the motive which impels them—the desire to do right—is precisely the same. The circumstances which govern their actions change, and their conduct must conform to the new order of things.

Robert E. Lee

General Lee, born on this day in 1807, wrote the above to a friend after the Civil War.

JANUARY 20

One of the most natural, most common and most disastrous attitudes toward life is a negative reaction to trouble. . . . It's nonsense to call an untroubled life the ideal. What can an untroubled life know about living? How can that help anybody? Dr. Harry Emerson Fosdick

In one of his sermons Dr. Fosdick told of how Marie Antoinette "played with life" until trouble struck. Then, he said, "She who had lived like a fool came to her end like a queen." "Tribulation," said she, "first makes one realize what one is."

JANUARY 21

He who finds a thought that lets us penetrate a little deeper into the eternal mystery of nature has been granted great grace. He who, in addition, experiences the recognition, sympathy and the help of the best minds of his time, has been given almost more happiness than a man can bear. Albert Einstein

JANUARY 22

Basic to an integrated and over-coming life is a domi-nant ideal. . . . To plow a straight row one must keep his eye on the goal rather than on the plow.　　J. M. Price.

JANUARY 23

God himself is a primal humorist. . . . The Christian faith is very funny. (It is also very solemn but that is not in dispute.) By laughter we acknowledge the human con-dition and get outside the solitary prison of self.

Chad Walsh

Mr. Walsh has a jolly poem about a stodgy good man who made much of his puny, unimaginative sins and his re-pentance. He finally died—just "as he expected, not wel-comed home nor finally rejected." He stayed in purgatory a long time, the inference being that they didn't want him in heaven because he was such a bore. Then a new spirit, "newly come and reeking still of nicotine and rum," told him a good story about the farmer's daughter.

"He laughed. He paled. He laughed again. The water
Of clear humility rained down his skin,
Dissolved the lucent sheath of subtle sin.
(St. Peter's sides were aching when he let him in.)"

JANUARY 24

A wise man will make haste to forgive because he knows the true value of time and will not suffer it to pass away in unnecessary pain. Samuel Johnson

JANUARY 25

There is another very safe and simple way of escape when the dull mood begins to gather round one and that is to turn as promptly and as strenuously as one can to whatever work one can do at the moment. Through humbly and simply doing what we can, we retrieve the power of doing what we would. Francis Paget

JANUARY 26

To be angry is to revenge the fault of others upon ourselves. . . . Act nothing in furious passion. It's putting to sea in a storm.   Alexander Pope

The little book *One Day at a Time in Al-Anon*, published for the families of alcoholics, both in and out of Alcoholics Anonymous, again and again warns the sober person against allowing anger and resentment over the acts of the alcoholic to take hold of him. They are, says Al-Anon, a boomerang which returns impatience and hostility to the sender. It quotes Jonathan Swift: "Whoever is out of patience is out of possession of his soul. Men must not turn into bees who kill themselves in stinging others."

JANUARY 27

They fail, and they alone, who have not striven.
                    Thomas Bailey Aldrich

JANUARY 28

Keep the faculty of effort alive in you by a little gratu-itous exercise each day. That is, be systematically ascetic or heroic in little unnecessary points, do every day or two something for no other reason than that you would rather not do it, so that when the hour of dire need draws nigh, it may find you not unnerved and untrained to stand the test. William James

JANUARY 29

Prayer is a force as real as terrestrial gravity. As a physician I have seen men, after all therapy failed, lifted out of disease or melancholy by the serene effort of prayer. Only in prayer do we achieve that complete and harmonious assembly of body, mind and spirit which gives the frail human need its unshakable strength.

Dr. Alexis Carrel

Prayer is one of life's most puzzling mysteries. I have sometimes feared it is presumptuous to take up God's time with my problems. Limit your prayers to requests for guidance, an open mind to receive it, and fortitude to act upon it, say some wise people. The Reverend Hal Daniel, an Episcopal clergyman I admire very much, has another view. The Lord's Prayer, he points out, is as specific as bread and debt.

JANUARY 30

*I believe a leaf of grass is no less
than the journey-work of the stars.*

. . .

*And a mouse is miracle enough
to stagger sextillions of infidels.*

Walt Whitman

JANUARY 31

Lord, receive our supplications for this house and family. Prolong our days in peace and honor. Give us health, food, bright weather and light hearts.

Robert Louis Stevenson

FEBRUARY 1

Has thou entered into the treasures of the snow? Or hast thou seen the treasures of the hail? . . . By what way is the light parted, which scattereth the east wind upon the earth? Who hath divided a watercourse for the overflowing of waters, or a way for the lightning of thunder; To cause it to rain on the earth, where no man is; on the wilderness wherein there is no man; To satisfy the desolate and waste ground; and to cause the bud of the tender herb to spring forth? Hath the rain a father? Or who hath begotten the drops of dew? Out of whose womb came the ice? And the hoary frost of heaven, who hath engendered it? . . . Canst thou bind the sweet influences of Pleiades, or loose the bands of Orion? . . . Canst thou send lightnings, that they may go and say unto thee, Here we are? Job 38:22–35

February is a weather month. Even in the South, where I live, it is wonderful, terrible, full of caprice and surprises. It's a time for weather poetry and I know of none more stirring than the Lord's speech to Job out of the whirl-wind.

FEBRUARY 2

Goodness is the only investment that never fails.
                                    Henry David Thoreau

FEBRUARY 3

The wise man is the experienced man who lives with his eyes and his heart wide open, full of reverent wonder and radical amazement. . . . He lives so wakefully and expectantly that little of value escapes his notice and whatever is worthwhile evokes his loving attention. He sees the things of this world as rare treasures or as things never seen before.   William McNamara

FEBRUARY 4

We can change any situation by changing our internal attitude toward it.   Dr. Harry Emerson Fosdick

FEBRUARY 5

There is nothing, sir, too little for such a creature as man. It is by studying little things that we attain the great art of having as little misery and as much happiness as possible. Samuel Johnson

For a start, study the sunlight. It's different every day, every hour, every season. April sunlight is a green-gold elixir like dandelion wine or lemonade but February's is something else, pale as sourwood honey and fragile.

There's a lovely comparison of the sunlight in a book by Frederic Prokosch called the *Age of Thunder*. In France, says a character, the sunshine is "clear and sweet and yet spiced with antiquity." In England, "golden but too elusive . . . colors fade and retire." In Spain, "hard and brutal, brown and yellow and red, with a gash of darkness" like a cave. In Italy, "hard but with a certain resilience and glamour," trembling on the leaves in Tuscany and casting "hot grape-colored shadows."

Imagine walking forth into the sunlight and not noticing.

FEBRUARY 6

It's not men's acts which disturb us . . . but it is our own opinions which disturb us. No wrongful act of another brings shame to thee.   Marcus Aurelius

FEBRUARY 7

O, God, teach me how to disagree without being disagreeable.   Father James Keller

FEBRUARY 8

My text is chilblains. . . .   Alice Hegan Rice

So often in life we reach for people where they aren't, speak to them about matters they have neither the ear nor the inclination to hear. Alice Hegan Rice's Mrs. Wiggs of the Cabbage Patch knew better. When she attempted to teach a Sunday school lesson to a group of hungry, ragged slum children she remembered the army chaplain who was going to preach to freezing soldiers huddled around a weak campfire. He saw their misery and he addressed it: "My text is chilblains. . . ."

FEBRUARY 9

If, at the end of each day, a person could look back on three tiny acts of self-denial, he would already be on the way to a happy inner life.   Bishop Fulton J. Sheen

FEBRUARY 10

Nobody ever FINDS life worth living. One always has to MAKE it worth living.   Dr. Harry Emerson Fosdick

FEBRUARY 11

There is a time in every man's education when he arrives at the conviction that envy is ignorance; that imitation is suicide; that he must take himself for better, for worse, as his portion; that though the wide universe is

full of good, no kernel of nourishing corn can come to him but through his toil bestowed on that plot of ground which is given to him to till.   Ralph Waldo Emerson

Unfortunately, in February, the month that the seed catalogues begin to come, Emerson does not literally mean that you are free to get outdoors and clear away dead stalks and make ready for spring planting. The furrow you have to plow, the plot given you to till, might be at a desk inside a building.

FEBRUARY 12

There are men as good as he, but they do bad things. There are men as intelligent as he, but they do foolish things. In him goodness and intelligence combined and made their best result in wisdom. . . . May God make us worthy of the memory of Abraham Lincoln!

Phillips Brooks

The celebrated Episcopal bishop from Massachusetts was in Philadelphia when Abraham Lincoln's body lay in state in Independence Hall, on April 23, 1865. His eulogy of the slain President is one of the finest I have read.

FEBRUARY 13

A man's age is as unimportant as the size of his shoes if his interest in life is not impaired, if he is compassionate and if time has mellowed his prejudices.

Oliver Wendell Holmes

FEBRUARY 14

The test of religion, the final test of religion, is not religiousness but love—not what I have done, not what I have believed, not what I have achieved, but how I discharged the common charities of life.

Dr. Henry Drummond

A sermon for Valentine's Day.

FEBRUARY 15

The foolish and the dead alone never change their opinions.   James Russell Lowell

FEBRUARY 16

As the marsh-hen secretly builds on the watery sod,
Behold, I will build me a nest on the greatness of God.
                                                    Sidney Lanier

He's an old-fashioned poet, and schoolchildren, even schoolchildren in Georgia, his home state, are no longer required to memorize the works of Sidney Lanier. But I can't visit the coast and see the beautiful marshes of Glynn County without remembering his poem about them.

"Ye marshes, how candid and simple and nothing-withholding and free," he wrote, offering them up for us to emulate. "Ye publish yourselves to the sky and offer yourselves to the sea."

FEBRUARY 17

Training is everything. The peach was once a bitter al-
mond; cauliflower is nothing but cabbage with a college
education.   Mark Twain

FEBRUARY 18

It's not your dog. It's God's dog.

Robert Louis Stevenson

There's a reticence, a kind of pseudopoliteness in most of us that makes us avert our faces when we see cruelty and injustice. We don't want to get involved. Then it's well to remember the story about Robert Louis Stevenson. He saw a man beating a dog unmercifully. When he intervened, the man said angrily, "It's *my* dog!" Mr. Stevenson's beautifully involved retort was: "It's not your dog. It's God's dog. And I am here to protect it!"

FEBRUARY 19

Stress is a part of living and it is necessary to deal with it.

Dr. Arnold A. Hutschnecker

FEBRUARY 20

*Men need work for the good of their souls as well as for
the good of their pocketbooks and all the pension schemes
on earth won't alter that fundamental human necessity.*

Elsie Robinson

FEBRUARY 21

What is lovely never dies,
But passes into other loveliness,
Star-dust, or sea-foam, flower or winged air.

Thomas Bailey Aldrich

FEBRUARY 22

*First in war, first in peace and first in the hearts of his
countrymen he was second to none in the humble and en-
dearing scenes of private life. Pious, just, humane, tem-
perate and sincere; uniform, dignified and commanding,
his example was edifying to all around him as were the*

effects of that example lasting. . . . Correct throughout, vice shuddered in his presence and virtue always felt his fostering hand; the purity of his private character gave effulgence to his public verities.

Henry Lee, father of General Robert E. Lee, is the source of the schoolchild's standard "first-in-war" Washington's Birthday speech. (Do young ones still chant, "First in war, first in peace, first in the hands of the chief of police"?) Lee wrote the speech on the occasion of Washington's death; it was delivered on December 26, 1799.

FEBRUARY 23

Those men who lack both courage and temperance are guided through life as donkeys are by the stick they fear and the carrot they long for, and they live a donkey's life, not the life of a man.　　　　　　　Stringfellow Barr

FEBRUARY 24

Anger blows out the lamp of the mind.
　　　　　　　　　　　　Robert G. Ingersoll

FEBRUARY 25

Intermittency—an impossible lesson for human beings to learn. How can one learn to live through the ebb-tides of one's existence? How can one learn to take the trough of the wave? . . . Perhaps this is the most important thing. . . . Simply the memory that each cycle of the tide is valid; each cycle of the wave is valid; each cycle of relationship is valid.   Anne Morrow Lindbergh

FEBRUARY 26

Indolence is a virtue. It comes from two Latin words, which mean freedom from anxiety or grief. And that is a wholesome state of mind. There are times and seasons when it is even a pious and blessed state of mind, not to be in a hurry; not to be ambitious or jealous or resentful; not to feel envious of anybody; not to fret about today nor worry about tomorrow—that is that way we ought to feel; that is the kind of indolence to encourage in ourselves.

Dr. Henry Van Dyke

FEBRUARY 27

Suffering, accepted and vanquished, will give you a serenity which may well prove the most exquisite fruit of your life. Cardinal Mercier

FEBRUARY 28

My hands evoke sight and sound out of feeling . . .
They give color to the honeyed breeze
The measure and passion of a symphony
To the beat and quiver of unseen wings.
In the secrets of earth, sun and air,
My fingers are wise;
They snatch light out of darkness.
They thrill to harmonies breathed in silence.

Helen Keller

Helen Keller did not consider herself a poet but nobody ever wrote more feelingly of the senses of touch and smell. Deaf and blind from babyhood, mute until she was sixteen, she saw light and heard harmonies unknown to most of us. In her book *The World I Live In* (The Century Company, 1908), she writes not of darkness but of "the delicate tremble of a butterfly's wings in my hand, the soft petals of violets curling in the cool folds of their leaves or lifting sweetly out of the meadow grass; the clear, firm outline of face and limb; the smooth arch of a horse's neck, the velvety touch of his nose."

FEBRUARY 29

Bless to us the pleasures, bless to us the pains of our existence. Watch upon our eyes, ears, thoughts, tongues and hands that we may never think unkindly, speak unwisely nor act unrighteously.   Sir Francis Bacon

MARCH 1

Full many a glorious morning have I seen
Flatter the mountaintops with sovereign eye,
Kissing with golden face the meadows green,
Gilding pale streams with heavenly alchemy.

William Shakespeare

MARCH 2

Everything looks so fresh and green and promising that I am beginning to feel gay and kittenish like a colt in a barley patch. Joel Chandler Harris

Some people, old-fashioned ones who believe in such ancient rites, are propelled into mighty, earth-shaking orgies of house cleaning in March. The author of the Uncle Remus stories in a letter to his daughter, written March 20, 1898, expressed a contrary view:

"If I were a housekeeper I wouldn't live in a house that had to be turned upside down every day to get the dirt out of it. A genuine spring cleaning means that Chloe and Johnson and John and Lizzie and Rufus and Banks and Ca'line are to come in to the tune of one of Sousa's marches played on the piano by Essie, tear up the carpets, knock down the plastering, break the clocks and drop a stove on the back porch. Mama has made no attempt as yet to sun the bathtub but I'm expecting it every day. When it happens I'm going to have the chimneys taken down and dusted. When this is done I'm going to have the woodpile cleaned and polished and then I'm going to have all the dirt swept out of the garden. I think a clean garden—a garden with no dirt at all in it—is one of the loveliest sights on earth."

MARCH 3

Georgia soil is so rich that when we throw corn to the chickens they have to catch it on the fly or eat it off the stalk.   Nunnally Johnson

MARCH 4

This great nation will endure as it has endured, will revive and will prosper. So, first of all, let me assert my firm belief that the only thing we have to fear is fear itself —nameless, unreasoning, unjustified terror, which paralyzes needed efforts to convert retreat into advance.

Franklin D. Roosevelt

The words were spoken in President Roosevelt's first inaugural address, March 4, 1933, but they have been repeated in one context or another many times since.

MARCH 5

Do good with what thou hast or it will do thee no good.
William Penn

MARCH 6

Scar tissue is the strongest skin of all. Kites and airplanes rise against the wind, not with it. Earth does not reveal its harvest without plowing, nor minds their treasure without study, nor nature its secrets without investigation. The defect, overcome, may become the greatest strength. Bishop Fulton J. Sheen

MARCH 7

Safety is not to be found in searching for the line of least resistance. Winston Churchill

MARCH 8

*Man's restless yearning to give something of himself,
whether it be a physical child or a spiritual child—the
child of his mind—a bridge, a poem, a song, an invention,
a cure for disease—is the true answer to all cynics and
pessimists who maintain that man is total selfishness.*

Rabbi J. R. Liebman

MARCH 9

*Consider how much more pain is brought on us by
anger and vexation . . . A good disposition is invincible, if
it be genuine.*   Marcus Aurelius

All the sages, ancient and modern, counsel rooting out
anger and resentment in the interest of self-preservation,
if for no other reason. To counteract our urge to criticize
and nurse our grievances, Al-Anon urges its members to
borrow a device from Alcoholics Anonymous' famous
Twelve Steps. Step Number Four: Make a searching and
fearless inventory of ourselves. "Perfection," says Al-

Anon, "is a long way off but improvement can be made to happen every day."

MARCH 10

I have a dream today . . . I have a dream that one day every valley shall be exalted, every hill and mountain shall be made low. The trough place will be made plain, and the crooked place will be made straight. And the glory of the Lord shall be revealed, and all flesh shall see it together. This is our hope. This is the faith that I go back to the South with. With this faith we will be able to hew out of the mountain of despair a stone of hope. With this faith we will be able to transform the jangling discords of our nation into a beautiful symphony of brotherhood. With this faith we will be able to work together, to stand for freedom together, knowing that we will be free one day. Martin Luther King, Jr.

A black man with a Bible in his hand, a vision and stubborn goodness in his heart, brought about America's greatest revolution since that first one two hundred years ago.

MARCH 11

The only way to get rid of sin is to quit it right now.
                                    Bishop Warren Akin Candler

When I was a new reporter on the Atlanta *Constitution* they sent me out to interview the celebrated Methodist bishop Warren Akin Candler, on his eighty-fifth birthday. He was an old man and ill but there was something about his snapping eyes and feisty speech that later sent me to reading his biography and his sermons. The bishop, a man of deep-dyed, fighting orthodoxy, considered observance of the Sabbath "indispensable to the moral, social, economic and political life of the nation." He preached about it constantly and one day he learned that his brother Asa, the founder of the Coco-Cola Company, was embarking on a business trip on Sunday.

Asa attempted to explain it with a biblical allusion. "It's a case of the ox in the ditch, Warren," he said. "No, Asa," said the bishop. "It's a case of the jackass in the sleeping car."

I go back often to his sturdy, no-foolishness but ever-hopeful utterances such as this one: "In the long run only the good can possibly survive."

MARCH 12

Trust thyself. . . . The virtue in most request is con-
formity. . . . I am ashamed to think how easily we capit-
ulate to badges and names, to large societies and dead
institutions. . . . I do not wish to expiate, but to live. My
life is for itself and not for a spectacle.

Ralph Waldo Emerson

MARCH 13

You must walk like a camel, which is said to be the only
beast which ruminates when walking.

Henry David Thoreau

Thoreau considered it a dull, housebound day if he failed
to walk four hours, seeking ever a different route and
walking not so much to exercise the body as the mind. He
took his text from Wordsworth, whose servant was asked
to show a visitor the poet's study. "Here is his library,"
said the servant. "But his study is out of doors."

MARCH 14

Weep like a willow, mourn like a dove,
You can't get to heaven 'thout you go by love.

Negro Spiritual

MARCH 15

Youth never shows its glorious vividness and vitality so much as when transfiguring monotony. I still feel a very strong and positive pleasure in being stranded in queer, quiet places where nothing happens and anything might happen. . . . It seems as if we needed such places and sufficient solitude in them to let certain nameless suggestions soak into us and make a richer soil of the subconsciousness.

G. K. Chesterton

MARCH 16

Green grows the laurel and so does the rue,
Sugar is sweet but not like you;
And since it is no better, I'm glad it's no worse,
Brandy in my bottle and money in my purse.

Old Ballad

MARCH 17

We would often be sorry if our wishes were gratified.

Aesop

Sometimes it's easy to identify with the old laborer of the fable. He was so tired of gathering sticks in the forest he thought he could bear life no longer, and he cried out for Death to come and take him. As he spoke, Death, a grisly skeleton, appeared and said, "What wouldst thou, Mortal? I heard thee call me." The woodcutter had reconsidered. "Please sir," he said, "would you kindly help me lift this faggot of sticks on to my shoulder?"

MARCH 18

*Our greatest happiness . . . does not depend on the
condition of life in which chance has placed us, but is
always the result of a good conscience, good health, occupation and freedom in all just pursuits.*

Thomas Jefferson

MARCH 19

*Sweet are the thoughts that savor of content
The quiet mind is richer than a crown;
Sweet are the nights in careless slumber spent;
The poor estate scorns fortune's angry frown.
Such sweet content, such minds, such sleep, such bliss
Beggars enjoy, when princes oft do miss.*

Robert Greene

MARCH 20

*We are here and it is now; farther than that all human
knowledge is moonshine.*   H. L. Mencken

Everybody advises us to live one day at a time but it's not so easy. Fears of tomorrow and guilt over yesterday haunt us all. The Al-Anons make it a part of their creed, saying: "Just for today, I will live through this day only, and not tackle all my problems at once. I can do something for twelve hours that would appall me if I felt I had to keep it up for a lifetime."

MARCH 21

The courage of life is often a less dramatic spectacle than the courage of the final moment. . . . A man does what he must, in spite of personal consequences, in spite of obstacles and dangers and pressures, and that is the basis of all human morality.   John F. Kennedy

MARCH 22

What a man knows at 50 that he did not know at 20 is, for the most part, incommunicable. . . . The knowledge he has acquired with age is not the knowledge of formulas, the forms of words, but of people, places, actions—a knowledge not gained by words but by touch, sights, sound, victories, failures, sleeplessness, devotion, love—the human experiences and emotions of this earth and of one-self and other men; and perhaps, too, a little faith, a little reverence for things you cannot see.   Adlai Stevenson

MARCH 23

There are many persons ready to do what is right because in their hearts they know it is right. But they hesitate, waiting for the other fellow to make the first move. . . . The minute a person whose word means a great deal dares to take the open-hearted and courageous way, many others follow.   Marian Anderson

MARCH 24

. . . Work is never done while the power to work remains. . . . For to live is to function. That is all there is to living.

Oliver Wendell Holmes on his ninetieth birthday

MARCH 25

I love best to have each thing in its season, doing without it at all other times. I have never got over my surprise that I should have been born into the most estimable place in all the world, and in the nick of time, too.

Henry David Thoreau

MARCH 26

I do not know what I may appear to the world but to myself I seem to have been only like a boy playing on the sea-shore, and diverting myself in now and then finding another pebble or a prettier shell than ordinary, whilst the great ocean of truth lay all undiscovered before me.

Isaac Newton

Albert Einstein was himself a simple, humble man and he admired these qualities in the master, Isaac Newton. Not what he had done but what was left to be done engrossed him and he liked to quote the same sentiment expressed by Newton.

MARCH 27

Sweet mercy is nobility's true badge.

William Shakespeare

MARCH 28

The ways along which we have to struggle toward the goal may be veiled in darkness. Yet the direction in which we must travel is clear. We must reflect together about the meaning of life. We must strive together to attain a theory of the universal affirmation of the world and life.

Dr. Albert Schweitzer

MARCH 29

Six Ways to Tell Right from Wrong

1. Submit the problem to the test of common sense. Don't be silly! 2. Submit it to the test of sportsmanship. Are you

playing the game? Cheating? 3. Submit to the test of your best self, not the passionate self, not the careless or greedy self but the best self. 4. Submit it to the test of public opinion. "To keep clear of concealment, keep clear of the need of concealment," advised Phillips Brooks. "It's an awful hour when the first necessity of hiding anything comes." 5. Submit to the test of the personality you admire most. 6. Submit to the test of foresight. Where is it coming out?

Condensed from Dr. Harry Emerson Fosdick's
The Hope of the World.

MARCH 30

Short words are the best, and the old words, when short, are best of all.   Winston Churchill

MARCH 31

Lord, I shall be verie busie this day;
I may forget Thee, but doe Thou not forget me!

General Sir Jacob Astley before the
Battle of Edge Hill

APRIL 1

I have never been able to school my eyes
Against young April's blue surprise.

C. L. O'Donnell

APRIL 2

The most beautiful experience we can have is the mysterious. It is the fundamental emotion that stands at the cradle of true art and true science. Albert Einstein

APRIL 3

All work is as seed sown; it grows and spreads, and sows itself anew. Thomas Carlyle

APRIL 4

To fight aloud is very brave,
But gallanter, I know,
Who charge within the bosom
The cavalry of woe.

Emily Dickinson

APRIL 5

The grass flames up the hill sides like a spring fire . . .
as if earth sent forth an inward heat to greet the returning
sun; not yellow but green is the color of its flame; the sym-
bol of perpetual youth, the grass blade, like a long green
ribbon, streams from the sod into summer.

Henry David Thoreau

APRIL 6

Where thou art Obliged to speak, be sure to speak the
Truth; for Equivocation is half way to Lying as Lying, the
whole way to Hell. William Penn

APRIL 7

Late on the third day, at the very moment when, at sunset, we were making our way through a herd of hippopotamuses, there flashed upon my mind, unforeseen and unsought, the phrase, "Reverence for Life." The iron door had yielded; the path in the thicket had become visible. Now I had found my way to the idea in which affirmation of the world and ethics are contained side by side! Now I knew that the ethical acceptance of the world and of life, together with the ideals of civilization contained in this concept, has a foundation in thought.   Albert Schweitzer

APRIL 8

In everything worth having, even in pleasure, there is a point of pain or tedium that must be survived so that the pleasure may revive and endure.   G. K. Chesterton

APRIL 9

God is required for gayety. . . .

Bishop Fulton J. Sheen

The atheist, the agnostic, the skeptic, the materialist, all have to take themselves seriously, says this churchman, and self-exaltation "without a recognition of the mercy of God" may beget despair. He predicts that on the Last Day, "when the good Lord comes to judge the living and the dead, He will give a very special gift to those who have not taken either themselves or the world too seriously."

APRIL 10

In quietness and in confidence shall be your strength.

Ralph Waldo Emerson

APRIL 11

The only limit to our realization of tomorrow will be our doubts of today. Let us move forward with strong and active faith. Franklin D. Roosevelt

The night before he died at the Little White House in Warm Springs, Georgia, President Roosevelt wrote the above in a speech he planned to deliver over the radio to Jefferson Day dinners which would take place around the country. The day after his death, April 13, 1945, Steve Early, his press secretary, distributed copies of the undelivered speech to newspapermen in Atlanta.

APRIL 12

Example is the best precept. Aesop

Before any of us is tempted to lift his voice in criticism of others it is well to remember the fable of the mama crab who took her child walking on the sandy beach. I like it as much for the stately dialogue as for the lesson. "Child,"

said the mother crab, "you are walking very ungracefully.
You should accustom yourself to walking straight forward
without twisting from side to side." And the young one
replied: "Pray, Mother, do but set the example yourself
and I will follow you."

APRIL 13

*Nothing can work damage to me except myself, the
harm that I sustain I carry about with me and never am a
real sufferer except by my own fault.*

Ralph Waldo Emerson

APRIL 14

*What is defeat? Nothing but education, nothing but the
first step to something better.*   Wendell Phillips

APRIL 15

*We are speaking of love. A leaf, a handful of seed—
begin with these, learn a little what it is to love—*

First, a leaf, a fall of rain, then someone to receive
*   what a leaf has taught you, what a fall of rain*
*   has ripened.*
No easy process, understand; it could take a lifetime,
*   it has mine and still I've never mastered it—*
I only know how true it is: that love is a chain of
*   love, as nature is a chain of life.*

                                     Truman Capote

APRIL 16

I think this is the most extraordinary collection of tal-
ent, of human knowledge . . .   John F. Kennedy

Thomas Jefferson was an April child and one of the most delightful things I ever read about him was said by President Kennedy in a speech to Nobel Prize winners in 1962: "I think this is the most extraordinary collection of talent, of human knowledge, that has ever gathered together at the White House, with the possible exception of when Thomas Jefferson dined alone."

APRIL 17

One hard thing to realize is that people can be different from us without being crude, crooked or crazy.

Red Gray

APRIL 18

These two
Were the most nobly mannered men of all;
For manners are not idle, but the fruit
Of loyal nature and noble mind.

Alfred, Lord Tennyson

King Arthur and Sir Launcelot were the two "nobly mannered" of whom Tennyson spoke. It's very likely that their manners consisted not so much of social behavior as of kindness and grace toward all people in all walks of life. Sometimes we need to be reminded to show courtesy toward the people closest to us, the members of our own family.

APRIL 19

To live content with small means; to seek elegance rather than luxury, and refinement rather than fashion; to be worthy, not respectable, and wealthy, not rich; to study hard, think quietly, talk gently, act frankly; to listen to stars and birds, to babes and sages, with open heart; to bear all cheerfully, do all bravely, await occasions, hurry never. In a word, to let the spiritual, unbidden and unconscious, grow up through the common. This is to be my symphony. William Henry Channing

APRIL 20

Hark, I hear a blue bird sing
And that's a sign of coming spring.
The bullfrog bellers in the ditches
He's throwed away his winter britches.

. . .

The water warm, the weather fine,
The time has come for hook and line,
Adown the creek, around the ponds,
Are gentlemen and vagabonds.

And all our dirty little sinners
Are digging bait and catching minners.
The dogwood buds are now a-swelling,
And yaller jonquils sweet are smelling.
The little busy bees are humming
And everything says spring is coming.

Bill Arp

In Georgia there's a little town named for Bill Arp, although that was not a real name but the pseudonym of a man named C. H. Smith, an officer in the Confederate Army and a lawyer. For many years he wrote a column in the Atlanta *Constitution,* celebrating such pleasures as were left to the impoverished South and making some of the pains bearable by poking fun at them. In 1884 he observed wryly: "There are some things . . . that won't let you forget 'em, and when they come and go they leave you humbled and hacked and meek as a lamb with his legs tied. They take away your pride and your brag and your starch and your stiffening."

APRIL 21

The same degree in which man's mind is nearer to
freedom from all passion, in the same degree also is it

nearer to strength; and as the sense of pain is a charac-
teristic of weakness, so also is anger. For he who yields to
pain and he who yields to anger, both are wounded and
both submit.   Marcus Aurelius

APRIL 22

*Lord, help me to accomplish great things for Thee by
doing the little things that lie at hand.*

Father James Keller

APRIL 23

*The Mole had been working very hard all the morning,
spring-cleaning his little home. First with brooms, then
with dusters; then on ladders and steps and chairs, with a
brush and a pail of whitewash; till he had dust in his
throat and eyes, and splashes of whitewash all over his
black fur, and an aching back and weary arms. Spring was
moving in the air above and in the earth below and
around him, penetrating even his dark and lowly little
house with its spirit of divine discontent and longing. It
was small wonder, then, that he suddenly flung down his
brush on the floor, said "Bother!" and "O blow!" and also*

"Hang spring-cleaning!" and bolted out of the house without even waiting to put on his coat. Something up above was calling him imperiously, and he made for the steep little tunnel which answered in his case to the gravelled carriage-drive owned by animals whose residences are nearer to the sun and air. So he scraped and scratched and scrabbled and scrooged, and then he scrooged again and scrabbled and scratched and scraped, working busily with his little paws and muttering to himself, "Up we go! Up we go!" till at last, pop! his snout came out into the sunlight, and he found himself rolling in the warm grass of a great meadow.

"This is fine!" he said to himself. "This is better than whitewashing!"

Kenneth Grahame, the opening paragraphs
of *The Wind in the Willows*

APRIL 24

A fire was lighted in my heart.

Rose Hawthorne Lathrop

Nathaniel Hawthorne's redheaded daughter, Rose, was a selfish and headstrong young woman in her youth. But in her middle years, after an often unhappy marriage, she went to visit her former seamstress, who was dying in a basement on Blackwells Island, a sort of depot for the destitute sick. Revulsion and sympathy would not allow her to forget what she saw and in 1896 she opened a three-room nursing home for cancer victims over a bankrupt saloon on the Lower East Side. After the death of her husband, she became Mother Alphonsa, founder of the Dominican Order of St. Rose of Lima, and the cancer homes in New York, Atlanta, and several other cities are an outgrowth of her devotion and the love and dedication she inspired in other women. She took her motto from St. Vincent de Paul: "I am for God and the poor."

APRIL 25

Don't talk to me about the "illusions" of memory. Why should what we see at the moment be more "real" than what we see from ten years' distance? It is indeed an illusion to believe that the blue hills on the horizon would still look blue if you went to them. But the fact that they are blue five miles away and the fact that they are green when you are on them, are equally good facts.

C. S. Lewis

APRIL 26

That man may last but never lives
Who much receives but nothing gives,
Whom none can love, whom none can thank—
Creation's blot, creation's blank.

Bishop Warren Akin Candler

APRIL 27

Dost thou love life? Then do not squander time, for that is the stuff life is made of.   Benjamin Franklin

APRIL 28

Use your experience to advantage. Become wise by it. Make wisdom out of your hurt. Then it will cease to hurt you.   Sirio Esleve

APRIL 29

I will not be afraid;
I will not be afraid.
I will look upward
And travel onward
And not be afraid.

Chinese Song

The Chinese are said to have kept their courage up with this song during their long war with Japan. It's also a good one to remember for tomorrow, April 30, "a night of demons," according to ancient legend. On this night, witches and warlocks and all kinds of evil spirits were said to be loose in the world. Houses had to be purified with juniper, cowsheds protected by bouquets of herbs hung over the door, and the church bells were rung loudly to frighten off unearthly visitors.

APRIL 30

Give me my scallop-shell of quiet,
My staff of faith to walk upon,
My scrip of joy, immortal diet,
My battle of salvation
My gown of glory, hope's true gage,
And thus I'll make my Pilgrimage.

Donald B. Aldrich

MAY 1

The early morning has gold in its mouth.

Benjamin Franklin

MAY 2

Spring rides no horses down the hill,
But comes on foot, a goose-girl still.
And all the loveliest things there be
Come simply, so, it seems to me.

If ever I said, in grief or pride,
I tired of honest things, I lied;
And should be cursed forevermore
With Love in laces, like a whore,
And neighbors cold, and friends unsteady,
And Spring on horseback, like a lady!

Edna St. Vincent Millay

A spring month by rights, May is almost summertime warm in the South—a time of opulent, buxom beauty and fragrance. Magnolias come into bloom, swamps are a tangle of yellow jessamine, the air is busy with winged traffic —bluebirds and martins and the stylish brown thrasher. When I was a child in south Alabama, no matter how many warm days we had in March and April, you did not go swimming until the first of May. There was a rule, too, about not taking off your shoes and walking home from school barefoot. But naturally we violated that one. A child can't properly feel the warm pulse of the earth and the turn of the seasons except through the soles of his bare feet.

MAY 3

There never was a possum born that didn't find a 'simmon tree somewhere.   Bill Arp

The old-time Atlanta *Constitution* columnist quoted a neighbor named Cobe as saying that. "Cobe," he wrote, "has a chunk of a cow and a sow and pigs and about enough old rickety furniture to move in one wagon load . . . His face is three colors and splotched about and his mouth is in a twist one way and his nose in another and he is hump-shouldered and walks pigeon-toed but he don't care. . . . He works hard and always says he's getting along 'tolable' and finds no more trouble in supporting six children than he did one. Says he's raising his boys more for endurance than for show."

MAY 4

Man is an experiment, the other animals are another experiment. Time will show whether they were worth the trouble. Mark Twain

MAY 5

I believe that unarmed truth and unconditional love will have the final word in reality. That is why temporary defeat is stronger than evil triumphant.
Martin Luther King, Jr.

MAY 6

*O Lord, let us not live to be useless; for Christ's sake.
Amen.*   John Wesley

MAY 7

*Create for yourselves an auxiliary task, a simple and, if
possible, a secret one. Open your eyes and try to see
where a man needs a little time, a little sympathy.*

Albert Schweitzer

MAY 8

I wish I was in Dixie, hooray, hooray . . .

Daniel Decatur Emmett

Southerners stand up, as do most Americans, when "The
Star-Spangled Banner" is played. It is a conscientious, on-
purpose response, solemn and respectful. But when the

band plays "Dixie" they come to their feet spontaneously, emotionally, clapping hands, stamping feet, and sometimes yelling exuberantly. "Dixie," of course, has more bounce and beat than that other national anthem but it isn't much easier to sing. And, oddly enough, most of us have never known all the words which Daniel Decatur Emmett put together for his minstrel tune so many years ago. We settle for the lines about "Injun batter," living and dying in Dixie, and a lot of joyful "look-aways," whatever they mean. But the rest of the lyrics (Cole Porter is turning over in his grave!) meander around, part nonsense, part charming imagery, for many stanzas. Omitting the "look-aways," I love these:

> The world was made in jis' six days,
> And finished up in various ways,
> They then made Dixie trim an' nice,
> And Adam called it "Paradise."
>
> · · ·
>
> Way down South in the fields of cotton,
> 'Simmon seed and sandy bottom!
> Then way down in the fields of cotton,
> Vinegar shoes and paper stockin's.

MAY 9

Self-indulgence is the law of death; self-denial is the law of life. Bishop Warren Akin Candler

MAY 10

Genius may conceive but patient labor must consummate.   Horace Mann

MAY 11

Duty is the sublimest word in our language. Do your duty in all things. You cannot do more. You should never do less.   Robert E. Lee

Duty is not a word that gets much wear and tear in my vocabulary. It sounds so unpleasant—and I've generally been in the fortunate position of enjoying what I had to do. My smart, conscientious son-in-law, however, might have a different view. He professes to be appalled at the way my children and I have avoided math all our lives. He quotes us as saying with outrageous and unbecoming pride, "*We* don't do math!" He's right and maybe I'll live to regret it but so far I've put math in a class with the castor oil I haven't taken and the alligators I haven't wrestled. If it had been a real duty . . . well, I wouldn't have called it "sublime" but I might have muddled through on my mother's oft-repeated assurance: "You *can* do what you *have* to do."

MAY 12

How a resentment, while it lasts, draws one back and back and back to nurse and fondle and encourage it! It behaves just like a lust.   C. S. Lewis

MAY 13

For I am persuaded, that neither death, nor life, nor angels, nor principalities, nor powers, nor things present, nor things to come,
Nor height, nor depth, nor any other creature, shall be able to separate us from the love of God, which is in Christ Jesus our Lord.   Romans 8:38–39.

After many days by the bedside of someone who was in a coma and dying, I became obsessed, even tortured, by the question of his whereabouts. The man I had known and loved was not in that body with the straps holding it to the bed and the tubes running into it. But between apparent death and actual death where does the person go? Where is the fine intelligence, the laughter, the love? I stood by the window and searched the sky, listened to labored breathing, waiting and questioning. The person, the essential person, had to be *somewhere*. Dr. Wallace Alston, a brilliant and kind Presbyterian minister, who was later to become president of Agnes Scott College, came to see me in the absence of my own minister, who was out of town. A minister should know, I thought, and I asked him the question. To his everlasting credit he gave me no quick and easy answer. He did not know, he said. But he did know something—and he quoted the above two verses from the Bible. They eased my aching unknowing then and they have eased and comforted me through the years since.

MAY 14

When the stars was all a-tremble
In the dreamin' field o' blue
An' the daisy in the darkness
Felt the fallin' o' the dew,
There come a sound o' melody
No mortal ever heard
An' all the birds seemed singin'
From the throat o' one sweet bird!
Then the other birds went Mayin'

In a land too fur to call;
For there warn't no use in stayin'
When one bird could sing for all!

Frank L. Stanton

MAY 15

There is a perennial nobleness, even sacredness, in work. Were a man so benighted or forgetful of his high calling, there is always hope in him who actually and earnestly works; in idleness alone there is perpetual despair.

Thomas Carlyle

MAY 16

It has been my lot in life, living in the wilderness as I do, to be out in storms a great many times. I never knew one that did not do me good. For a storm, whether it be physical or spiritual, is always a challenge; and there is something in the heart that rises up to meet it.

Archibald Rutledge

MAY 17

Much has been determined for you by causes beyond your control; your circumstances, your inheritance, your talents; but one thing has not been determined and that is what use you will make of them.   Dr. Henry Van Dyke

MAY 18

Naked and alone we came into exile.

. . .

Which of us has known his brother?
Which of us has looked into his father's heart?
Which of us has not remained forever prison-pent?
Which of us is not forever a stranger and alone?

. . .

Remembering speechlessly
We seek the great forgotten language,
The lost lane-end into heaven,
A stone, a leaf, an unfound door.

Thomas Wolfe

MAY 19

Many are avidly seeking but they alone find who remain in continual silence. . . . Every man who delights in a multitude of words, even though he says admirable things, is empty within. If you love truth, be a lover of silence.
Isaac of Nineveh

MAY 20

The idle mind will sometimes fall into contemplations that serve for nothing but to ruin the health, destroy good humor, hasten old age and wrinkles and bring on an habitual melancholy.
Mary Wortley Montagu.

An idle mind was not a problem with Mrs. Montagu. She was one of the great letter writers of the eighteenth century. People who advise us how to take hold of our lives are eternally advising letter writing. Dorothea Brande puts it in two of her twelve disciplines. Write a letter, she directs, without once using I, me, my, or mine. And later on she has you writing a "successful" letter—that is one that is cheerful and upbeat. But no lying is allowed. You have to look for something cheerful to say. I checked out Mrs. Montagu's letters to her fiancé in 1711, and Dorothea Brande would have been proud of her. No self-engrossment, no whining about, but brisk and lively news of the day, philosophy, and humor.

MAY 21

We shall see what great hope there is that death is good. For death must be one of two things; either he who is dead becomes as naught and has no consciousness of anything; or else, as men say, there is a certain change and a removal of the soul from this place to some other. Now if there be no consciousness and death be like a sleep in which the sleeper has no dreams, then were it a wonderful gain indeed . . . But if death be a transition to another place, and if it be true that all who have died are there, what, O judges, could be greater good than this?

Socrates to his judges

MAY 22

Sometimes they're in the corner, sometimes they're by the door.

Sometimes they're all a-standing in the middle
of the floor;
Sometimes they are a-sittin' down, sometimes
they're walkin' round
So softly and so creepy-like they never make a
sound!
Sometimes they are as black as ink, an' other
times they're white—
But the color ain't no different—when you see
things at night!

Eugene Field

As a child I took "expression." (An earlier generation called it "elocution.") Besides boring my friends and neighbors to death with my recitations, I know of nothing the lessons accomplished except that I memorized Eugene Field's "Seein' Things at Night." After childhood "ghoulies and ghosties and long-leggety beasties and things that go bump in the night" aren't the problem. But most of us see other things—mistakes and problems and old and new griefs—and they all look their absolute worst in the middle of the night. It helps sometimes to say *Seein' Things at Night* to yourself and to know that many of the fears and worries are as imaginary as they were in childhood.

MAY 23

O Lord, I cannot plead my love of Thee.
I plead thy love of me.
The shallow conduit hails the unfathomed sea.

Christina Rossetti

MAY 24

Frugality is good if Liberality be join'd with it.
William Penn

MAY 25

Take heart, there are things more precious than politi-
cal victory; there is the right of political contest. And who
knows better how vigorous and alive it is than you who
bear the fresh, painful wounds of battle? Adlai Stevenson

MAY 26

Ideas are always disturbing, especially new ideas. Most normal, charming, intelligent adults have learned to leave their minds alone and so are immune to new ideas. But not gardeners. These unfortunates are susceptible to every new idea carried by the wings of chance.

Josephine Nuese

The author of one of my favorite books, *The Country Garden,* calls this susceptibility "divine discontent" in the gardener. I wonder if it could be carried over into the human condition. Planting daffodils under the oak tree sounds a lot easier than beautifying and expanding a squinchy mind and spirit.

MAY 27

Old age—Let us embrace it, let us love it. To him who knows how to use it, it is full of enjoyment . . . the absence of all want is itself a sort of pleasure . . . How sweet it is to have lived out and taken leave of all anxious desires!

Seneca

MAY 28

There is no use making the same mistake twice when there are so many new ones you can make.   Red Gray

MAY 29

I dread success. To have succeeded is to have finished one's business on earth, like the male spider, who is killed by the female the moment he has succeeded his courtship. I like a state of continual becoming, with a goal in front and not behind.   George Bernard Shaw

MAY 30

The truth is incontrovertible. Panic may resent it; ignorance may deride it; malice may distort it. But there it is.
Winston Churchill

MAY 31

God be in my head and in my understanding;
God be in my eyes and in my looking;
God be in my mouth and in my speaking;
God be in my heart and in my thinking;
God be at mine end and at my departing.

Eastern Prayer

JUNE 1

And what is so rare as a day in June?
Then, if ever, come perfect days;
Then Heaven tries earth if it be in tune,
And over it softly her warm ear lays.
Whether we look, or whether we listen,
We hear life murmur, or see it glisten;
Every clod feels a stir of might,
An instinct within it that reaches and towers,
And, groping blindly above it for light,
Climbs to a soul in grass and flowers.

James Russell Lowell

The Vision of Sir Launfal as a long narrative poem was wasted on me as a teen-ager. I can't remember the story. The whole thing seems to blend with those other tedious tomes, *Silas Marner* and *The Lady of the Lake*. But the oft-quoted little scrap of poetry about June has stuck with me all these years, giving me something to declaim lustily when I walk about the garden and find that, in truth, those little seeds I planted have groped for the light and are climbing to a soul. Whatever else he said, Mr. Lowell said that just right.

JUNE 2

There is an urgency in April and May in both man and nature, an urgency that quiets during June. The promises of early spring are fulfilled this month. . . . Now, in June all courses and winter commitments have ended. . . . We can thin our weeks even further and frequently for a day, for an hour, do nothing—just nothing at all.   Jean Hersey

JUNE 3

Courage, cowardice, ferocity, gentleness, fairness, justice, cunning, treachery, magnanimity, cruelty, malice, malignity, lust, mercy, pity, purity, selfishness, sweetness, honor, loyalty, falsity, veracity, untruthfulness—each human being shall have all of these in him and they will constitute his nature. In some there will be high and fine characteristics which will submerge the evil ones and those will be called good men; in others the evil characteristics will have dominion and those will be called bad men. God speaking in Mark Twain's "Letter from the Earth."

JUNE 4

A time of prosperity is a dangerous time; the soul loafs and grows fat. Archibald Rutledge

JUNE 5

A little rebellion now and then is a good thing and as necessary in the political world as storms in the physical. Thomas Jefferson

JUNE 6

I had to go to Valdosta.   W. H. Smellie

People have written books about the efficacy of saying
"No." You don't have to do everything everybody asks you
to do, sacrifice your time and energy to every random
request. Just say "No." My neighbor, Winston H. Smellie,
called Doc, seldom refuses any request, reasonable or un-
reasonable. He is a source of encouragement, help, tools,
and refreshment in every earth-shaking project we under-
take. When he doesn't pitch in on something we all grin
and tell one another that he had to go to Valdosta, a little
town two hundred miles to the south of us.

It's Doc's story. When he had an office in the city,
where he worked for thirty years before retiring to the
country, he knew an old man who manufactured some
wings and sold them, at great expense, to a group of black
church people who wanted to fly to heaven. The take-off
was set for a Sunday afternoon from the roof of a two-
story building on the edge of town. There the people
gathered with their wings strapped to their shoulders;
there they jumped and there they fell, breaking legs and
arms right and left. Doc later saw the wing merchant and
asked him what he did when his customers started plum-
meting to the ground.

"I wasn't there," the man said. "I had to go to Valdosta."

JUNE 7

Forgiveness has a vision which allows the aggrieved to view his predicament from outside himself. Now the aggrieved says, "He, too, suffers. He, too, is ignorant and guilty. He, too, is driven contrary to better judgement." As this insight congeals into conviction, they find friends in their enemies.   Sirio Esleve

JUNE 8

Physical bravery is an animal instinct; moral bravery is a much higher and truer courage.   Wendell Phillips

JUNE 9

I heard somewhere that if you can't have the best of everything, make the best of everything you have.
     Red Gray

JUNE 10

Eat and drink such an exact quantity as the constitution of thy body allows of, in reference to the services of the mind. They that study much, ought not to eat so much as those that work hard, their digestion being not so good. Excess in all other things whatever, as well as in meat and drink, is also to be avoided. . . . The difficulty lies in finding out an exact measure; but eat for necessity, not for pleasure for lust knows not where necessity ends.

Benjamin Franklin

JUNE 11

No one makes his way through the world scot-free. Every man has his Waterloo and his Dunkirk; it is how we stand up to them that makes all the difference.

Samuel M. Silver

JUNE 12

Return the Civilities thou receivest, and be grateful for Favors.   William Penn

JUNE 13

Easy conditions frequently put the soul to sleep, while hard conditions stir the soul to strive for the highest things which otherwise might be neglected.

Bishop Warren Akin Candler

JUNE 14

The four freedoms of common humanity are as much elements of man's needs as air and sunlight, bread and salt. Deprive him of a part of these freedoms and he dies —deprive him of a part of them and a part of him withers. Give them to him in full and abundant measure and he

will cross the threshold of a new age, the greatest age of man.   Franklin D. Roosevelt

Flag Day, June 13, 1942

JUNE 15

Anyone who proposes to do good must not expect people to roll stones out of his way.   Albert Schweitzer

JUNE 16

We must then control our thoughts and our desires. We must acquire interior freedom . . . so that we are able to use the good things of life and able to do without them for the sake of higher ends. It means the ability to use or to sacrifice all created things in the interests of love.

Thomas Merton

The monastic life of prayer, meditation and work must appeal to all of us at some point in our lives. When I visit the Trappist monastery on the old farm place, which once belonged to actress Colleen Moore a few miles south of Atlanta, I come away impressed by the radiance on the faces of the people there. (I usually go to gloat over and covet the plants in Father Paul's greenhouse but occasionally to visit the starkly simple and altogether beautiful chapel, which the monks built with their own hands.) They work hard, sleep on spartan boardlike beds, eat the plainest food, have no worldly goods, and are up and at prayers in that cold chapel at all hours of the night. And yet they have a serenity and a happiness that has sent me more than once searching for understanding in the books of Thomas Merton, who became a monk himself.

"The climate in which monastic prayer flowers is that of the desert," he wrote in *Contemplative Prayer*, "where the comfort of man is absent, where the secure routines of man's city offer no support and where prayer must be sustained by God in the purity of faith. Even though he may live in a community, a monk is bound to explore the inner waste of his own being as a solitary."

JUNE 17

Rootless, hopeless, workless urban poverty is the greatest single cause of misery in the world.

Adlai Stevenson

JUNE 18

Blessed is he who has found his work; let him ask no other blessedness.   Thomas Carlyle

JUNE 19

We thank Thee for the joy of common things,
The laughter of a child, the vagrant grace
Of water, the great wind that beats its wings,
The sudden light that shines upon a face.

.   .   .

To strengthen for this day's huge and harsh demanding
We thank Thee, Lord; for patience yet to find
A brave new hope, a brave new understanding
In the vast commonwealth of heart and mind.

Joseph Auslander

JUNE 20

One ought, every day at least, to hear a little song, read a good poem, see a fine picture, and, if it were possible, to speak a few reasonable words. Goethe

Of the four—song, poem, picture, and words—the last is undoubtedly the most difficult. My neighbor, the late Lum Crow, saw only the poems and pictures in nature, which he knew well, and, banjo in hand, he made his own songs. But he was rich in calmness and reasonableness and so self-effacing that when they took him to the hospital, shortly before his death, he put on his hat and tried to leave in his pajamas and slippers. "You got all your people a-visiting," he said apologetically to a nurse. "I don't want to put you out none; I'll just go on down the road."

JUNE 21

You give but little when you give of your possessions. It is when you give of yourself that you truly give. Kahlil Gibran

JUNE 22

Failure is more frequently from want of energy than from want of capital.   Daniel Webster

JUNE 23

She swung the ax in a wide arc and it sank into the wood straight across the top of the head. . . . The wood, straight-grained and true, came apart with a crying, rendering sound, but stood for an instant longer like a thing whole, the bowed head, the shoulders; then slowly the face fell forward toward the ground. . . . The man reached for the fallen face. . . . He touched the wood where the face should have been, and nodded. "Christ yu meant it tu be—butcha couldn't find no face fu him." She shook her head below the lifted ax. "No. They was so many would ha done; they's millions an millions a faces plenty fine enough—fer him." She pondered, then slowly lifted her glance from the block of wood, and wonder seemed mixed with the pain. "Why, some a my neighbors down there in th' alley—they would ha done."

Harriette Arnow

Harriette Arnow's book *The Dollmaker* is so real and so true that after I sent it to my mother to read I realized I did not want her to be alone when she reached the death of a child in it. I got in the car and drove 250 miles to be with her in what I knew would be grief and pain. Gertie, the Kentucky mountain woman uprooted and thrust into the confusion of wartime Detroit, has a lot to tell us about conformity and adjusting as she lives in a city slum and longs for her mountain home. But the final passage, where she gives up her beloved block of cherry wood upon which she had been carving, to be sawed into boards for cheap, money-making dolls, would be unbearable except for one thing. Gertie realizes that the poor, fearful, driven people who were her neighbors bore the face she had been seeking to carve—the face of Christ.

JUNE 24

I am the voice of one crying in the wilderness. Make straight the way of the Lord. . . . I baptize with water but there standeth one among you whom ye know not. He it is, who coming after me is preferred before me, whose shoe's latchet I am not worthy to unloose.

John 1:23, 26–27

In the Christian calendar, June 24 is marked as the birthday of John the Baptist. Whether it was actually his birthday no one knows, but because he was called "a burning and shining light," it seemed suitable to choose his birthday as a celebration on Midsummer's Day, to replace the old pagan Midsummer Eve. The pagan worship centered on the sun and included bonfires and dancing and the uses of ashes as charms against witchcraft and disease.

JUNE 25

Paste it up where you'll remember it: You could be wrong!   My mother, Muv.

Oliver Cromwell put it another way: "I beseech ye, in the bowels of Christ, think it possible that you may be mistaken!"

JUNE 26

I find the great thing in this world is not so much where we stand, as in what direction we are moving; to reach the port of heaven, we must sail sometimes with the wind and sometimes against it—but we must sail, and not drift and not lie at anchor.   Oliver Wendell Holmes

JUNE 27

Slander slays three persons; the speaker, the listener and the one who is being slandered. Talmud

JUNE 28

We see extraordinary and unexampled proofs of Divine favour. The sea has been divided; the cloud has attended you on your way; the rock has flowed with water; the manna has rained from heaven; everything has concurred to promote your greatness. What remains to be done must be done by you; since in order not to deprive us of our free will and such share of glory as belongs to us, God will not do everything Himself. Niccolò Machiavelli

JUNE 29

A thing moderately good is not so good as it ought to be. Moderation in temper is always a virtue, but moderation in principle is always a vice. Thomas Paine

JUNE 30

*Teach us, O Lord, the disciplines of patience, for we
find that to wait is often harder than to work. May we be
willing to stop our feverish activities and listen to what
Thou hast to say, that our prayers shall not be the sending
of night letters, but conversations with God.*

Peter Marshall

JULY 1

*Time is dissolved, it blows like a little dust:
Time, like a flurry of rain,
Patters and passes, starring the window-pane.*

Conrad Aiken

JULY 2

*It's a wonder to me that everybody don't go to farming.
Lawyers and doctors have to set about town and play*

checkers and talk politics and wait for somebody to quarrel or fight or get sick; clerks and bookkeepers figure and multiply and count . . . the jeweler sits by his window all year round working on little wheels and the mechanic strikes the same kind of lick every day. These people don't belong to themselves; they are all penned up like convicts in a chaingang; they can't take a day or an hour for recreation for they are the servants of their employers. There is no profession that gives a man such freedom, such latitude and such variety of employment as farming.

Bill Arp

JULY 3

At the present time when violence . . . dominates the world more cruelly than it ever has before, I still remain convinced that truth, love, peaceableness, meekness and kindness are the violence that can master all other violence.　　　　　　　　　　　Albert Schweitzer

JULY 4

To all true men the birthday of a nation must always be a sacred thing.　　　　　　　　　　　Phillips Brooks

On July 4, 1879, the Episcopal bishop of Massachusetts was invited to preach in Westminster Abbey before Queen Victoria. He undoubtedly felt that because almost a hundred years had elapsed since the United States won her freedom from England it would not be tactless to exult a little in his country's riches and opportunities. "On my country's birthday," he said, "I may ask for your prayers in her behalf. That on the manifold and wondrous chance which God is giving her—on her freedom (for she is free since the old stain of slavery was washed out in blood); on her unconstrained religious life, on her passion for education and her eager search for truth; on her zealous care for the poor man's rights and opportunities; on her quiet homes where the future generations of men are growing, on her manufactories and her commerce; on her wide gates open to the west; on her strange meeting of the races out of which a new race is slowly being born; on her vast enterprise and her illimitable hopefulness—on all these materials and machineries of manhood, on all the life of my country must mean for humanity, I may ask you to pray that the blessing of God, the father of men, and Christ, the son of men, rest forever."

JULY 5

"We talked the matter over and could have settled the war in thirty minutes had it been left to us."

Bell Irvin Wiley

The war was the Civil War and the soldier quoted was a Confederate who had sat and chatted for half an hour with a Yankee enemy in the woods. According to Dr. Wiley, a distinguished Civil War historian, now retired from Emory University, it wasn't at all unusual for Johnny Reb and Billy Yank to visit back and forth across the trenches, to swap goods and socialize, and on many occasions to play or sing their music together. All this to the consternation of their officers. Dr. Wiley records in his book *The Life of Johnny Reb* occasions where a truce was declared so they might bury their dead together. I always choke up over accounts of their music fests. Once at Fredericksburg, Virginia, during the war's second winter, a crack group of Union musicians posted on the northern bank of the Rappahannock began playing a medley of patriotic northern airs and war songs. "Now give us some of ours," shouted the Confederates across the river.

"Without hesitation the band swung into the tunes of 'Dixie,' 'My Maryland,' and the 'Bonnie Blue Flag,'" wrote Dr. Wiley. "This brought forth a lusty and prolonged cheer from the Southerners. Finally the music swelled into the tender strains of 'Home, Sweet Home' and the countryside reverberated with the cheers of thousands of men on both sides of the stream."

It makes you wonder if the plain foot soldiers of any war couldn't have settled the differences without a fight—and why harmony is sometimes so difficult between individuals.

JULY 6

We all bear scars. Life is a struggle and hurts must come. . . . It behooves us to travel softly, regardful of one another's happiness, particularly where our path crosses that of those dependent upon us for comfort or enters into the hearts of little children.   Anonymous

JULY 7

A good conscience is a continual Christmas.
Benjamin Franklin

JULY 8

The virtuous would seem to think that they have a privilege to make themselves disagreeable, whereas in them ill-temper is doubly a vice.
Bishop J. L. Spalding

When I told my longtime friend, Jack Spalding, editor
of the Atlanta *Journal*, that I was putting together a book
of daily quotations which cheered or comforted or chided
me he told me about the *Spalding Year Book* which a lady
named Minnie R. Cowan assembled in 1905 from the
writings of his kinsman, Bishop Spalding. It is apparently
a member of a large company of such books because it is
labeled "Helpful Thought Series." I love the little book
and have borrowed from it freely, rejoicing in the fact
that Bishop Spalding, as the magazine *The Ave Maria*
said at the time, "never points out an evil or sounds a
warning without suggesting a remedy." So many pointers-
out of evil fail here.

JULY 9

*Work helps to preserve us from three great evils—
weariness, vice and want.*   Voltaire

JULY 10

*If man has not found something he will die for he is not
fit to live. . . . I do not know what will happen to me
now and it really does not matter. . . . I am not old. Like*

*any man I would like a long life but am not concerned
about that now. I just want to do God's will. . . . And he
has allowed me to go up to the mountain top . . . and I
have looked over and I have seen the Promised Land
. . . and I may not be able to lead you all the way, but
mine eyes have seen the glory of the coming of the Lord.*

Martin Luther King, Jr.

JULY 11

*The weak and the ignorant are quickest to threaten and
punish. And it is only where teachers lack moral and intel-
lectual power that they resort to harsh measures.*

Bishop J. L. Spalding

JULY 12

*More often than not we don't want to know ourselves,
don't want to depend on ourselves, don't want to live with
ourselves. By middle life most of us are accomplished
fugitives from ourselves.*   John W. Gardner

JULY 13

When Andrew Jackson, "Old Hickory," died, someone asked, "Will he go to Heaven?" and the answer was, "He will if he wants to." If I am asked whether the American people will pull themselves out of this depression, I answer, "They will if they want to."   Franklin D. Roosevelt

Americans heard that and took heart when President Roosevelt said it in his third "fireside chat" in July of 1933. It applies equally, I am sure, to personal depressions. We can pull ourselves out of them if we want to.

JULY 14

The most common things are the most useful; which shews both the Wisdom and Goodness of the Great Lord of the Family of the World. What therefore he has made rare, don't thou use too commonly: Lest thou shouldest invert the Use and Order of things; become Wanton and Voluptuous; and thy Blessings prove a Curse.
                                                    William Penn

JULY 15

I was angry with my friend:
I told my wrath, my wrath did end.
I was angry with my foe:
I told it not, my wrath did grow.

William Blake

JULY 16

The power of ideals is incalculable.   Albert Schweitzer

JULY 17

Simple folk are those who have accepted the truth as a
way of life and have thus avoided the complications of
false living.   Sirio Esleve

JULY 18

The most compelling and majestic element in our human nature is that which we call conscience. It is deathless. In age extreme, when appetite has grown dull and desire is dead, conscience will show itself strong and authoritative. Bishop Warren Akin Candler

JULY 19

I have read my epitaph so many times that I thought I was dead and then, when I wake up in the morning I find I am alive. It is a matter of delight, I must confess.
Adlai Stevenson

JULY 20

"Does the way I live really matter?" To ask the question, to inquire into life, to doubt the sensibility of existence, these are not questions of a disturbed and thwarted mind. These are questions that man will always ask, in

sickness and in health, because they are rooted in the organic pattern of life itself. And because man strives for the infinite, man will forever be frustrated and doomed to suffer. But in the suffering, in the struggle, in his loneliness and solitude, he achieves his individuality and his identity.   Clark E. Moustakas

JULY 21

Health lies in action. To be busy is the secret of grace, and half the secret of content. Let us ask the gods not for possessions but for things to do.   Will Durant

JULY 22

Men are like rivers. The water is alike in all of them; but every river is narrow in some places and wide in others; here swift and there sluggish, here clear and there turbid, cold in winter and warm in summer. Every man bears within himself the germs of every human quality, displaying all in turn.   Tolstoy

JULY 23

No religious teacher who has not himself tasted of the bitter cup of rejection, agnosticism and fear can be of help to other men and women.   Rabbi J. R. Liebman

JULY 24

Quien canta sus males espanta. He who sings frightens away his ills.   Miguel De Cervantes

My singing frightens away everything—and everybody. But I know exactly what Cervantes is talking about. Once many years ago a neighbor of my mother's called me to say that Muv had been stricken mysteriously ill and they were taking her to the hospital. I jumped in the car and took off—worried and frightened, of course, but managing to hold my real fear in abeyance by singing at the top of my voice all the way there. Hymns and love songs and the nonsense jingles of my children's days at camp came pouring out. My bellowing "Smoke Gets in Your Eyes" and "Jesus Wants Me for a Sunbeam" into the defenseless country air did not change the basic problem, of course, but there was something calming about it. My optimism and good humor at my mother's bedside surprised even me—and it was real.

JULY 25

I believe in the sun when it is not shining. I believe in love even when not feeling it. I believe in God even when he is silent.   Inscription in a Cologne
                          cellar where Jews hid

JULY 26

When power leads man toward arrogance, poetry reminds him of his limitations. When power narrows the areas of man's concern, poetry reminds him of the richness and diversity of its existence. When power corrupts, poetry cleanses.   John F. Kennedy

Robert Frost came often to Atlanta to speak at Agnes Scott College. I always went to hear him and usually interviewed him for the newspaper. Toward the end of his life he was sometimes forgetful and his mind would wander. But when he stood up to read his poetry his mind was sharp and clear. The last time he read *The Death of the Hired Man* there wasn't a dry eye in the auditorium.

JULY 27

Forge thy tongue on an anvil of truth
And what flies up, though it be but a spark,
Shall have weight.

Pindar

JULY 28

Touch the spirit of civilization by getting and master-ing great books. Fashion your tongue to high and noble speech and your mind to lofty thought.

Bishop Warren Akin Candler

Atlanta's long-time mayor, the late William B. Hartsfield, was a beautifully educated man who had very little schooling. When he had to drop out of high school, he wrote a dozen college presidents and asked them to send him a list of the twelve books they regarded as most important to a man's education. He read every book on every list and if it happened to be the choice of two college presidents he read it twice. He was a prime example of what Robert Frost told me once: When you learn to read and discover books you don't need any more schooling.

JULY 29

Do not despair. If you want to be different, you may. You, too, can be changed for the better. Therein lies our hope—and the hope of the world.   Peter Marshall

JULY 30

Man is a marvelous curiosity. When he is at his very very best he is a sort of low grade nickel-plated angel; at his worst he is unspeakable, unimaginable; and first and last and all the time he is a sarcasm.   Mark Twain

JULY 31

Give us, Lord, a bit o' sun
A bit o' work and a bit o' fun;
Give us all in the struggle and sputter
Our daily bread and a bit o' butter;
Give us health, our keep to make,
An' a bit to spare for others' sake.
Give us sense, for we're some of us duffers,
An' a heart to feel for all that suffers;
Give us, too, a bit of song
And a tale, and a book to help us along.
An' give us our share of sorrow's lesson
That we may prove how grief's a blessin'.
Give us, Lord, a chance to be
Our goodly best for ourselves and others
Till all men learn to live as brothers.

Inscribed on the wall of an old
inn in Lancaster, England

AUGUST 1

I am my own priest and I shrive myself
Of all my wasted yesterdays. Though sin

And sloth and foolishness and all ill weeds
Of error, evil and neglect grow rash
And ugly there, I dare forgive myself
That error, sin and sloth and foolishness.
God knows that yesterday I played the fool,
God knows that yesterday I played the knave.
But shall I therefore cloud this new dawn o'er
With fog of futile sighs and vain regrets?

. . .

This is another day—are its eyes blurred
With maudlin grief for any wasted past?
A thousand failures shall not daunt!
Let dust clasp dust; death, death—I am alive!
And out of all the dust and death of mine
Old selves I dare to lift a singing heart
And living faith; my spirit dares drink deep
Of red mirth mantling in the cup of morn.

Don Marquis

AUGUST 2

Religion, when you boil it down to a concrete, is nothing more than something to do, something to love and something to hope for.
Sam Jones

August used to be camp-meeting time in the South—a time when crops were laid by and families were free to hitch up their wagons and drive to Old Salem or Shiloh or New Hope campgrounds for a week of physical rest and spiritual refreshment. One of the most celebrated of the old-time revivalists was Sam P. Jones of Cartersville, Georgia. Mr. Jones was born in 1847 and educated to be a lawyer, but he took up strong drink and was headed for perdition, as he later claimed, when he had a religious conversion and took to preaching. (His grandsons, Howell and Paul Jones, long-time newspaper friends of mine, say that the evangelist probably never was the heavy drinker that he thought himself to be.) Anyhow, he became a powerful prohibitionist, preaching all over the country about the evils of drink and the power of salvation. "Nobody but an infernal scoundrel will sell whiskey and nobody but an infernal fool will drink it," he said. He was colorful and witty and outspoken and wherever he traveled and preached he drew vast enthusiastic audiences. He died in 1906 on his way home from conducting a revival in Arkansas. His body lay in state in Georgia's capitol, drawing an estimated 30,000 mourners. Recently, when I covered a murder trial in his home town of Cartersville, I visited the Sam Jones Memorial Baptist Church next door to the courthouse and during a recess drove a few blocks out to look at his home, a beautiful old house set in a square of woodland and grass surrounded by an iron fence. Landmark-loving citizens have a move afoot to save the house and turn it into a museum.

Sam Jones's sermons are probably museum pieces themselves nowadays, running heavily to denunciations of booze and "meanness," but I love to read them. Once he began preaching by holding up a piece of paper which he said somebody had put in the collection plate the night before. It read: "Brother Jones, I am in your debt as follows: For quitting and swearing off from drinking—one hundred dollars. For quitting and swearing off from swearing—one hundred dollars. For quitting all my meanness—one million dollars. For learning to love our dear Lord better than life—three billion dollars. Credit—one dollar. [He enclosed the dollar.] I hope to be able to pay the balance by doing good the remainder of my days."

AUGUST 3

One day in bluest of summer weather
Sketching under a whisper oak,
I heard five bobolinks laughing together
Over some ornithological joke.

C. P. Cranch

AUGUST 4

It is of the utmost importance that, in facing our de-
feats and failures, we shall never yield to discouragement;

for discouragement, from a spiritual point of view, is the result of wounded self-love and is therefore a form of pride.   Bishop Fulton J. Sheen

AUGUST 5

You are as young as your faith, as old as your doubt, as young as your self-confidence, as old as your fear; as young as your hope, as old as your despair.

Samuel Ullman (Muv's collection)

My mother, Muv, has an old book stuffed with clippings that she found in the barn at home fifty years ago. She doesn't know who clipped them and put them there or what publication they came from but she has saved them and read and reread them, finding some of them a yellowed and brittle distillation of wisdom. And some, like the one above, have been useful to others: General Douglas MacArthur had these words posted above his desk in Tokyo.

AUGUST 6

Whatever your occupation may be and however crowded your hours with affairs, do not fail to secure at

least a few minutes every day for refreshment of your inner life with a bit of poetry.   Charles Eliot Norton

AUGUST 7

You will find it less easy to uproot faults, than to choke them by gaining virtues. Do not think of your faults; still less of others' faults; in every person who comes near you, look for what is good and strong; honor that; rejoice in it; and, as you can, try to imitate it; and your faults will drop off, like dead leaves, when their time comes.

J. Ruskin (Muv's collection)

J. Ruskin is most certainly John Ruskin but Muv's old scrapbook doesn't call him that. It also skimps on space by calling Emerson "R. W." instead of Ralph Waldo, probably because one of its favorite sages is a man named M. A. Schimmelpenninck, a real space-user.

AUGUST 8

I remember only calling the Lord by his surname of Almighty and winding up by asking Him to confound our enemies and to send us help and friends. The last word es-

caped from me in a sob. . . . It was a great relief, these tears, and the feeling of having been perfectly frank with the Lord. . . . The whole thing sounds blasphemous but I suppose that is because our ideas of God are still shot through with superstition and a sort of cringing notion of deity. Corra Harris

Corra Harris was desperate on the day of which she wrote in *My Book and My Heart*, published in 1924. The wife of a Methodist minister, the Reverend Lundy Harris, she had just nursed him through a terrible time when he lost his religious faith and suffered a mental breakdown. He had no job, they were broke, and Corra sold all their household goods at auction in order to get money to live. When he was better and able to take a teaching job (at three hundred dollars a year!) Mrs. Harris reached some sort of turning point. She had never been as pious as he was. She once wrote that Lundy "had a nervous, flighty conscience and was always getting balled up in some scruple. I do not think he had enough moral elasticity." But she believed in God enough to follow her husband into church one day and wait until he had said his prayers and left. Then she said hers, crying out her pain and all but demanding God's help. It came. Some small magazine pieces she had written were bought and published and her career as a popular and successful magazine writer and novelist was launched. Her most successful novel, *A Circuit Rider's Wife*, was made into a movie, which 20th Century-Fox shot in the Georgia mountains in the 1950s, calling it *I'd Climb the Highest Mountain*, starring Susan Hayward.

"I remember turning frantically to God, which I never do as long as I can keep my own nose above water," she wrote. "But I can recommend Him as a God who never failed me at such times. I have not been preserved from any sorrow because, I suppose, sorrow is good for growing souls. It is the dark side of great blessings. . . . But when I needed strength or courage for the weather ahead, I always received it."

AUGUST 9

My moments are flying,
Soon I shall be dying,
O let me then prize
My time as it flies.

And shall I sleep when rosy morn
Its light and glory sheds?
Immortal beings were not born
To rot in downy beds.

Shall birds and bees and ants be wise
Whilst I my moments waste?
O let me with the morning rise
And to my duty haste.

Back in 1844 there was no television violence to warp the minds of little children, but they did have "Uncle Charles" and his book *Simple Rhymes and Familiar Conversations,* published in Penfield, Georgia, by a local printer. He not only warned them about dying with such couplets as:

> *"Come little children, think of death,*
> *And for the grave prepare"*

but he cautioned them against rotting in bed when there was duty awaiting. As an early riser myself, I love his preachments, but I won't push them on children in the family just yet.

AUGUST 10

Ideals are like stars; you will not succeed in touching them with your hands. But like the seafaring man on the desert of waters, you choose them as your guides, and following them you will reach your destiny.   Carl Schurz

AUGUST 11

There are people who are always anticipating trouble, and in this way they manage to enjoy many sorrows that never really happen to them.   Josh Billings

AUGUST 12

*Let us all resolve—First to attain the grace of silence;
Second to deem all fault-finding that does no good a sin,
and to resolve, when we are happy ourselves, not to poison
the atmosphere for our neighbors by calling on them to
remark every painful and disagreeable feature of their
daily life; Third, to practise the grace and virtue of praise.*

Harriet B. Stowe (Muv's collection)

AUGUST 13

*Man seems to be a rickety poor sort of a thing, any
way you take him; a kind of British Museum of infirmities
and inferiorities. He is always undergoing repairs. A ma-
chine that was as unreliable as he is would have no
market.*   Mark Twain

AUGUST 14

*All of us know that there are at large in the world
thousands of men and women of genius who never ac-*

complish anything because they are not handicapped by poverty.   Archibald Rutledge

AUGUST 15

Tim was so learned that he could name a horse in nine languages. So ignorant that he bought a cow to ride on.
                                   Benjamin Franklin

AUGUST 16

Blessed is he who lets his women impose on him, for it's better to submit to a little family dictation than to be an austere man. . . . I never say nay, provided it don't cost anything hardly.   Bill Arp

It was lay-by time on the farm. Work had slacked off and Mrs. Arp and the girls wanted to have a frolic for the neighbors. They first had to have the permission of their husband and father, who reported that a party "wasn't as bad as a war, nor death, nor pestilence and didn't happen more than once in two or three years so I concluded to make the best of it."

AUGUST 17

All satisfaction in life is grounded in a regular recurrence of things about us. The rhythm of day and night, of the seasons, that of blossoms and fruits; all things the enjoyment of which is contingent upon periodicity—these are the basic stimuli of earthly life. The more receptive we are to those enjoyments, the happier we feel.   Goethe

AUGUST 18

His dress was of the oddest description. Generally even in the coldest weather he went barefooted but sometimes for his long journeys he would make himself a rude pair of sandals; at other times he would wear any cast-off covering he chanced to find—a boot on one foot and an old brogan or a moccasin on the other . . . His principal garment was made of a coffee sack in which he cut holes for his head and arms to pass through . . . He constructed a hat of pasteboard with an immense peak in front. Notwithstanding his ridiculous attire he was always treated with the greatest respect by the rudest frontiersman and, what is a better test, the boys of the settlement forbore to jeer at him.   W. D. Bailey

Of all America's folk heroes Johnny Appleseed may be my favorite. He didn't exert himself with feats of strength as John Henry and Paul Bunyan are said to have done— and furthermore he was real. A man named John Chapman who gathered seeds from the cider presses of western Pennsylvania to make apple orchards throughout the Midwest.

AUGUST 19

What does indicate the progress of a people? Churches? No. Schoolhouses? No. The way men and women live and think and aspire. . . . If these are wrong, all is wrong, and the nation will gallop to hell no matter how many railroads and factories they build.

Tom Watson

Before I came to Georgia all I knew of Tom Watson was a watermelon by that name—and a credit to him it was too, that watermelon. It didn't take me long to learn that he was one of America's most fascinating, most exciting, and dangerous and paradoxical figures—a United States senator, the author of rural free delivery, the Populist Party's defeated candidate for vice-president of the United States, a lawyer, historian, newspaper editor, sometimes called a sage and sometimes a bigot and racist who "like a hydrophobic animal is snapping and biting at nearly everything." He lived from 1856 to 1922 and when he died the New York *Times* called him "a strange and vivid public character who already seems almost legendary." His statue is on the capitol lawn in Atlanta and when I pass that way I think about him and his many talents. He was a child during the Civil War but he never outgrew the conviction that the South should have been independent. To someone who doubted it, he cried: "Pluperfect bosh! Sickening servility! The quintessence of apostasy! The high-water mark of truckling self-abasement and lick-log propitiation!"

AUGUST 20

To me every hour of the light and dark is a miracle,
Every cubic inch of space is a miracle.

Walt Whitman

AUGUST 21

I am the inferior of any man whose rights I trample under foot. Men are not superior by reason of the accidents of race or color. They are superior who have the best heart—the best brain. Robert Ingersoll

AUGUST 22

It is defeat that turns bone to flint; it is defeat that turns gristle to muscle; it is defeat that makes men invincible.

Henry Ward Beecher

AUGUST 23

That man is richest whose pleasures are the cheapest.

Henry David Thoreau

AUGUST 24

Am I acting in simplicity, from a germ of the Divine life within, or am I shaping my path to obtain some immediate result of experience? Am I endeavoring to compass effects, amidst a tangled web of foreign influences I cannot calculate; or am I seeking simply to do what is right, and leaving the consequences to the good providence of God?

M. A. Schimmelpenninck (Muv's collection)

AUGUST 25

Do not be one of those who, rather than risk failure, never attempts anything.   Thomas Merton

AUGUST 26

When an American says that he loves his country, he means not only that he loves the New England hills, the prairies glistening in the sun, the wide and rising plains, the great mountains and the sea. He means that he loves an inner air, an inner light in which freedom lives and in which a man can draw the breath of self-respect.

Adlai Stevenson

AUGUST 27

When one wakes up after daylight one should breakfast; five hours after that, luncheon; six hours after luncheon, dinner. Thus one becomes independent of the

*sun, which otherwise meddles too much in one's affairs
and upsets the routine of work.*   Winston Churchill

Mr. Churchill seems to be changing his dependence from
the sun to a clock—and of the two, clock and sun, I prefer
the sun. But his schedule, fixed and immutable, would be
a delight to any cook.

AUGUST 28

*Content not thy self that thou art Virtuous in the gen-
eral; for one Link being wanting, the Chain is defective.
Perhaps thou are rather Innocent than Virtuous and owest
more to thy Constitution than thy religion. Innocent is not
to be Guilty: But Virtuous is to overcome our evil Inclina-
tions. If thou hast not conquer'd thy self in that which is
thy own particular Weakness, thou hast no Title to Virtue.*
            William Penn

AUGUST 29

*A man is ethical only when life, as such, is sacred to
him, that of plants and animals, as that of his fellowmen,*

and when he devotes himself helpfully to all of life that is in need of help.   Albert Schweitzer

AUGUST 30

August is ripening grain in the fields blowing hot and sunny, the scent of tree-ripened peaches, of hot buttered sweet corn on the cob. Vivid dahlias fling huge tousled blossoms through gardens and joe-pye-weed dusts the meadow purple.

Jean Hersey

AUGUST 31

This world is very lovely, oh my God. I thank thee that I live.   Bill Arp

SEPTEMBER 1

September is a sweep of dusky, purple asters, a sumac branch swinging a fringe of scarlet leaves, and the bitter-

sweet scent of wild grapes when I walk down the lane to the mailbox. September is a golden month of mellow sunlight and still clear days. . . . Small creatures in the grass, as if realizing their days are numbered, cram the night air with sound. Everywhere goldenrod is full out.

Jean Hersey

SEPTEMBER 2

One thing a father will never understand—why school must start so early in the day. Was it only yesterday that the world was quiet and a man could wake up and go in and put coffee on, and stand there yawning, with the bubble of the boiling water the only sound in the house? Brown and soaked by the summer sun, the kids slept on while the day brightened. Even the dog stayed asleep. A man could pour his coffee then, and go sit on the porch with never a stirring in the house to trouble him, never a peep of sound. Now peace is gone. In the cold dawn bells start ringing . . . there's a loud thump or two upstairs . . . the plumbing starts to roar . . . and the sound of violent altercations rises on the air. . . . Then down they come, feet thundering on the stair, and the foul ritual of breakfast takes place—a revolting sight in the early morning.

Harold H. Martin

Harold, who was my Atlanta *Constitution* office room-mate for many years, when he was not off covering wars and other world tempests and tremors for *The Saturday Evening Post*, could always write about children and dogs and cats and the dailyness of life better than anybody I knew. He once explained to me that the only excuse for writing about one's own children is that they are just like everybody else's children—a precept that relieved me of self-consciousness when I wrote about my own. It may not be exactly true but the way Harold writes you always feel he has caught old Universal Experience by the nape of the neck and the seat of the pants, all right. It never happened to me but I knew exactly how it was when he wrote: "Who put the BB's in the peanut butter?" taking a firm stand that a man "has a right to pick up a peanut-butter sandwich in his own house and bite down on it" without smashing up his bridgework "because some dope left a BB in the peanut butter."

SEPTEMBER 3

The mountaineer had the right idea when he refused the storekeeper's offer to try a banana, saying, "I've got more tastes now than I can satisfy." Periodically, every person needs to let go, not only a few days a year, a day or so a week but also a few hours a day and a few minutes every hour.   J. M. Price

SEPTEMBER 4

*I don't think much of dignity. My observation is that
the more dignity a man has the nearer dead he is.*

Sam Jones

The evangelist also pulls us up short on talking about the
past, a conversational turn I find very agreeable.

"Some fellows," says he, "are always talking about the
glorious past. They remind me of an old switch engine
with the headlight on the tender—throwing all the light
behind."

SEPTEMBER 5

*By nature we crave the symbolism of altars, the visible
images of invisible things.* Corra Harris

SEPTEMBER 6

"Damn it, holler them across!" General Jubal Early

Historian Bell Irvin Wiley, who has done more than anyone else to explore the character, personality, and situation of the common foot soldier in both the Confederate
and Union armies in the Civil war, has a story which, it
seems to me, is useful to the ill-equipped and the hard-
pressed at any time.

The "Rebel yell" was a famous cry in that war. Both
sides yelled, Dr. Wiley reports, but the Rebels' yell, being
wilder and more unearthly, was said to have struck terror
to their enemies' hearts the first time it was heard. Dr.
Wiley says it was "unpremeditated, unrestrained . . . a
mixture of fright, pent-up nervousness, exaltation, hatred
and a pinch of pure deviltry.

"Toward the end of an engagement near Richmond in
May 1864, General Early rode up to a group of soldiers
and said, 'Well, men, we must charge them once more and
then we'll be through,'" Dr. Wiley writes. "The response
came back, 'General, we are all out of ammunition.'
Early's ready retort was, 'Damn it, holler them across!'

"And," says the historian, "according to the narrator,
the order was literally executed."

In the sense that the Rebs' hollering was bluffing, I
guess we all holler ourselves through dilemmas and crises
when we have no other ammunition.

SEPTEMBER 7

*To hope is to risk frustration. Therefore, make up your
mind to risk frustration.*
                                      Thomas Merton

SEPTEMBER 8

Panics, in some cases, have their uses; they produce as much good as hurt. Their duration is always short; the mind soon grows through them, and acquires a firmer habit than before.   Thomas Paine

SEPTEMBER 9

We know nothing of to-morrow; our business is to be good and happy today.   Sydney Smith

SEPTEMBER 10

Those who dream by day are cognizant of many things which escape those who dream only by night.
                    Edgar Allan Poe

Since I was given *The Works of Edgar Allan Poe* for my sixteenth birthday I've cherished that quotation. Until Poe I did not know that daydreaming was useful. Most of the admonitions of my childhood were to "DO great deeds," not "dream them all day long." Poe suggested to me for the first time that a sufficiently enticing daydream created a blueprint for action.

SEPTEMBER 11

Perhaps middle age is, or should be, a period of shedding shells; the shell of ambition, the shell of material accumulations and possessions, the shell of the ego. Perhaps one can shed at this stage in life . . . one's pride, one's false ambitions, one's mask, one's armor . . . Perhaps one can at last in middle age, if not earlier, be completely oneself. And what a liberation that would be!

Anne Morrow Lindbergh

SEPTEMBER 12

There are so many small things that inspire:
The fragile note of lute instead of drum,
The frail star-jasmine clinging to its wire,
The dainty way a wren devours a crumb.
Wild arsenic's inverted china bowl
Contains enough perfume to bring delight—

A hummingbird can rest a weary soul,
And one small firefly cheer a lonely night.
Forever strange how small things touch the heart:
The unexpected handclasp of a friend,
The murmur of a brook, a dewdrop's art,
Or any rainbow's bright, elusive bend.
These strike as sudden hope on life's brief Lyre,
As when a farmer's hoe on flint sparks fire.

Marel Brown

Mrs. Brown is a friend of mine whose quick and unexpected little notes in the mail delight me as much as her poetry does. I think it is because she and her husband, Alex, persevere as gardeners, although they have twice built country homes and established country gardens and been forced to move because of subdivisions and developments. Now they have a bit of land with a stream and a barn on it—but no house—where they go daily in good weather to plant and savour earth's "small things."

SEPTEMBER 13

In loneliness some compelling essential aspect of life is suddenly challenged, threatened, altered, denied. At such times only by entering into loneliness, by steeping oneself in the experience and allowing it to take its course and to reveal itself, is there hope that one's world will achieve harmony and unity.   Clark E. Moustakas

SEPTEMBER 14

Tell me what you remember most easily and I will tell you what kind of person you are. Tell me what you keep stored in your memory and I will know fairly well whether you are coarse or cultured, whether you are scholarly or vulgar. What you treasure and keep as the permanent possession of memory is a good indication of what kind of person you are.   Bishop Arthur J. Moore

Bishop Moore did not store in his memory recollections of his own worth and achievements. At his funeral last summer I heard for the first time the best part of a story involving Bishop Moore that I covered years ago. A plane on which he, the most famous Methodist churchman in the world, was returning from California, caught fire and made a forced landing in a Kansas wheat field. The passengers were shaken up but unhurt, and I went to the airport with a photographer to meet and interview Bishop Moore when he arrived in Atlanta. He talked willingly and vividly of the plane's difficulties and of the courage of the crew and the other passengers. Not until I went to his funeral did I learn that the white-haired old bishop had been the one who struck out across the wheat field in the cold and the darkness toward the nearest light, looking for help for them all. He found a farmhouse and knocked. A woman opened the door and when the light fell on his face she cried, "Why, Bishop Moore, what are you doing here?" She was, of course, they all learned later, a Methodist minister's wife.

SEPTEMBER 15

Therefore it is well to let prayer be the first employment in the early morning and the last in the evening. Avoid diligently those false and deceptive thoughts which say, "Wait a little, I will pray an hour hence; I must first perform this or that." For such thoughts a man quits prayer for business, which lays hold of and entangles him so that he comes not to pray the whole day long.

Martin Luther

SEPTEMBER 16

A man who is constantly brooding over his rights inevitably thinks little of the rights of others and still less of his own duties to others. Bishop Warren Akin Candler

SEPTEMBER 17

No one should compel himself to show others more of his inner life than he feels is natural to show. . . . The only essential thing is that we strive to have light in ourselves. . . . Then we get to know each other as we walk together in the darkness, without needing to pass our hands over each other's faces, or to intrude into each other's hearts. Albert Schweitzer

SEPTEMBER 18

The want of due Consideration is the Cause of all Unhappiness Man brings upon himself. For his second Thoughts rarely agree with his first, which pass not without considerable Retrenchment or Correction. . . . Well may we say our Infelicity is of ourselves; since there is nothing we do that we should not do, but we know it and yet do it. William Penn

SEPTEMBER 19

Young beauty flowers on the shallow soil of the physical; spiritual beauty lays hold on the life-giving waters of eternal springs. Archibald Rutledge

SEPTEMBER 20

A fat kitchen makes a lean will. Benjamin Franklin

SEPTEMBER 21

The reading of poetry, with the spirit and the understanding . . . is in my judgment one of the very finest instruments for the opening of the mind, the enlarging of the imagination and the development of the character.
Dr. Henry Van Dyke

SEPTEMBER 22

Nothing else but this seeing God in everything will make us loving and patient with those who annoy and trouble us. Nothing else will completely put an end to all murmuring or rebelling thoughts.

H. S. Smith (Muv's collection)

SEPTEMBER 23

Why art thou troubled because things do not succeed with thee according to thy desire? Who is there who hath all things according to his will? Neither I, nor thou, nor any man upon earth. Thomas À Kempis

SEPTEMBER 24

For those of us who have lost our faith, or who have always had to struggle along without it, it is often helpful just to accept blindly and with no reservations. We need not believe, at first; we need not be convinced. If we can

*only accept, we find ourselves becoming gradually aware
of a force for good that is always there to help us.*

One Day at a Time in Al-Anon

SEPTEMBER 25

*I ask and wish not to appear
More beauteous, rich or gay.
Lord, make me wiser every year
And better every day.*

Charles Lamb

SEPTEMBER 26

*A slight sound at evening lifts me up by the ears and
makes life seem inexpressibly serene and grand. It may be
Uranus or it may be in the shutter.* Henry David Thoreau

Thoreau lived in a more peaceable, law-abiding age
when people did not lock their doors and worry about
noises in the night. It is still pretty much like that in the
country where I live. The nights are quiet except for an
occasional car on the road and the barking of the dogs.

There used to be two pine saplings growing up through the kitchen eaves and sometimes on a windy night they sighed and creaked like the rigging of a ship in a stiff breeze. They had to go when we added the porch and I miss them. I don't know how Uranus sounds but it could be that noise I thought was birds in the chimney is the stars wheeling and turning in their orbits.

SEPTEMBER 27

Civilization and violence are antithetical concepts, Negroes of the United States, following the people of India, have demonstrated that nonviolence is not sterile passivity but a powerful moral force which makes for social transformation. Sooner or later all the people in the world will have to discover a way to live together in peace and thereby transform this pending cosmic elegy into a creative psalm of brotherhood.
                Martin Luther King, Jr., accepting the Nobel Prize

SEPTEMBER 28

There is nothing more universally commended than a fine day; the reason is that people can commend it without envy.   Ralph Waldo Emerson

SEPTEMBER 29

To watch the corn grow and the blossoms set; to draw hard breath over ploughshare or spade; to read, to think, to love, to hope, to pray—these are the things that make men happy. . . . Now and then a wearied king, or a tormented slave, found out where the true kingdoms of the world were and possessed himself, in a furrow or two of garden ground, of a truly infinite dominion.   John Ruskin

SEPTEMBER 30

I'm glad I have a small soul,
That does not feel much pain.
It's pelted like an acorn
In a driving rain.

It is good to have a small soul
That cannot magnify the Lord.
The fullness of its total grief
Is encompassed in a word.

For if I had a huge soul
Like Francis Thompson had

The Hound of Heaven would search me out
And shake me till I'm dead.

John Strong

OCTOBER 1

In April mortal's eye hath seen
The waking woods arrayed in green,
While every birdling of the throng
Essayed sweet syllables of song.

And now October woos the wold
To dreams of crimson and of gold.
The laughing leaves all but out of breath
Are dancing down to dusty death.

Robert Loveman

Although he is known for one poem, *April Rain*, written in 1901 and popularized by Al Jolson in the 1920s ("It is not raining rain to me, It's raining vio-lets!"), Robert Loveman wrote and published in his lifetime (1864–1923) many volumes of beautiful verse. His old home in the little north Georgia town of Dalton is now used, appropriately enough, as a library.

OCTOBER 2

Not one of us knows what effect his life produces and what he gives to others; that is hidden from us and must remain so, though we are often allowed to see some fraction of it, so that we may not lose courage. The way power works is a mystery. Albert Schweitzer

OCTOBER 3

Out of my childhood I recall moments of pure magic, when some special loveliness laid its hand on my heart, never to leave it. I remember particularly a very special sort of April day, the day that I describe in the first chapter of "The Yearling." I remember the delirious excitement that I felt. And at the height of my delight, a sadness came over me, and I understood suddenly that I should not always be a child, and that beyond this carefree moment life was waiting with its responsibilities.

Marjorie Kinnan Rawlings

Mrs. Rawlings is describing the beginning inspiration for that lovely and special book, *The Yearling.* She goes on to tell how the idea for a story of a child's growing up remained in the back of her mind and was fleshed out when an old-timer in the Florida scrub told her of his love for a pet deer he had as a boy and how he was forced to shoot it when it leaped a fence and ruined the corn crop on which the livelihood of man and stock depended.

"All my life," the old man told her, "it's hurted me."

Once I spent most of a day with Mrs. Rawlings, covering a talk she made, interviewing her and seeing her later at a party the Atlanta Women's Press Club gave for her. She was a plain, fat, aging lady in a funny hat, but she seemed filled with deep, warm laughter and love for people who, since she was an Ohioan, must have been essentially foreign to her—the poor, uneducated Florida backwoodsmen I considered my own. I marveled that she knew and felt so much and set it down so truly. Later, in an introduction to a school edition of *The Yearling,* she lets us see that this understanding wasn't easily come by. She had meant to make Jody's mother the picture "of all nagging wives and mothers," but as she went on with the story, "I came to understand how hard life is for such a woman and how her sharp tongue hid the wounds in her own heart."

OCTOBER 4

He has either a mighty long head or a might short creed who believes only what he understands.

Sam Jones

OCTOBER 5

*There is really no such thing as adversity. It is a sort of
honorable degree the Lord confers upon you in living if
you have the quality and the courage to earn it.*

Corra Harris

OCTOBER 6

Captain, I want to make one change—a spire.

Martha Berry

Miss Berry, the renowned "Sunday lady from 'Possum
Trot," who started with a log cabin and a handful of poor
illiterate mountain children and founded the famous
Berry Schools outside Rome, Georgia, shocked her friend
and architect, Captain John Barnwell, by asking him to
put a steeple on the barn he designed for the Berry
campus. It would not be proper, the old gentleman told
her.

"Why do we put spires on churches?" Miss Berry asked,
and then answered herself. It was easy, she said, to be
mindful of God in a church on Sunday, but it was during

the week that her students, doing hard, hot, often monotonous labor, would need to have their hearts and spirits uplifted. She wanted spires on the barn and all the chicken houses.

"If they have a steeple it will catch their eye now and then and they'll think of God's blessings, including the blessing of having work to do," she said.

Martha Berry died in 1942 but to this day the outbuildings on the 30,000-acre scenic campus have steeples.

OCTOBER 7

It wouldn't be such a cold world if we'd make bonfires of the old stumbling blocks, and warm up to Happiness.
Frank L. Stanton

OCTOBER 8

A surplus of opportunities does not insure the best luck.
Henry Van Dyke

OCTOBER 9

I am a talker by inheritance. My father was an Irish-man and my mother was a woman. Henry W. Grady

Mr. Grady was truly a talker, what they used to call a silver-tongued orator. His statue down the street from our newspaper office says he "loved a nation back to peace" after the Civil War. His writing for the Atlanta *Constitution,* of which he was editor, spoke to the South, and his oratory spoke to the North. In one of his famous speeches, made to the New England Society in New York in 1886, Mr. Grady told a memorable story which illustrates eloquently the humor and the never-say-die spirit of a defeated people.

Two Confederate soldiers plodding home from Appomattox stopped by the roadside to roast some corn.

"You may leave the South if you want to," one tattered veteran remarked to the other, "but I'm going home to Sandersville, kiss my wife, raise a crop, and if the Yankees fool with me any more, I'll whip 'em again."

OCTOBER 10

*Once we have acquired the habit of inner attention, a
thousand truths come to us without our seeking. Life
develops from within, and he who would educate must
work upon the soul.*   Bishop J. L. Spalding

OCTOBER 11

*Gentleness and cheerfulness, these come before moral-
ity; they are the perfect duties. If your morals make you
dreary, depend upon it, they are wrong. I do not say give
them up, for they may be all you have; but hide them like
a vice lest they should spoil the lives of better and simpler
people.*   Robert Louis Stevenson

OCTOBER 12

*There is no limit to the good you can do if you don't
care who gets the credit for it.*   Elbert Hubbard

William B. Hartsfield, the late mayor of Atlanta, had a sign bearing these words prominently placed on the wall of his office. It was a gift to him from his long-time friend Robert W. Woodruff, the Coca-Cola magnate and philanthropist. Mr. Woodruff collected such words of wisdom himself. One poem, clearly original, follows.

OCTOBER 13

If your nose is close
To the grindstone rough,
And you hold it down
There long enough,
In time you'll say
There's no such thing
As brooks that babble
And birds that sing.
These three will all
Your world compose:
Just you, the stone
And your god-damned nose.

Bobby Jones

The late Grand Slam golfer and Atlanta lawyer sent that rhyme to Mr. Woodruff, who has been called one of the

ten richest men in the world. Presumably, Bobby Jones
thought his friend Bob Woodruff worked too hard.

Here is Mr. Woodruff's answer:

If you sing with the birds
And play in the brook
While the grindstone turns
'Gainst the other fellow's hook,
You'll find your place
At the table was took.

OCTOBER 14

*There is always a well-known solution to every human
problem—neat, plausible and wrong.*   H. L. Mencken

OCTOBER 15

Steal away, steal away,
Steal away to Jesus.
Steal away, steal away home.
I ain't got long to stay here.

My Lord He calls me,
He calls me by the thunder.
The trumpet soun' withina my soul,
I ain't got long to stay here.

Green trees a-bendin',
Po' sinner stan' a-tremblin',
The trumpet soun' withina my soul,
I ain't got long to stay here.

Negro Spiritual

The most haunting, most poignant song of my childhood in south Alabama was sung often by my black neighbors and friends. Years later I went out to Atlanta University to interview the black singer Roland Hayes. He told me the story of his personal fight against the inequities of segregation and he also told me that his grandfather, a slave on a Georgia plantation, was the author of my beloved "Steal Away." Religion and church services were forbidden to the slaves of that particular plantation but Mr. Hayes's grandfather had been converted to Christianity by a previous owner and he served as a preacher to the others. They had to meet secretly, when they met for services, and the way he assembled them was to start the song "Steal Away," and it was picked up gradually by every hand on the plantation.

That night when he finished his concert on the Woman's Club stage, Mr. Hayes gave "Steal Away" as an encore and dedicated it to me. It was the most beautiful thing I had ever heard and I went backstage to thank him with tears in my eyes.

OCTOBER 16

Great souls are brave souls and the wise understand that it is better to find fault with one's self than with one's country or one's age. Bishop J. L. Spalding

OCTOBER 17

If you confer a benefit, never remember it; if you receive one, never forget it. Chilon

OCTOBER 18

Speak when you are angry and you will make the best speech you will ever regret. Ambrose Bierce

OCTOBER 19

*If you know how to spend less than you get, you have
the philosopher's stone.*   Benjamin Franklin

OCTOBER 20

do not tell me
said warty bliggens
that there is not a purpose
in the universe
the thought is blasphemy

Don Marquis

Marquis' friend archy, the cockroach, and his pal mehi-
tabel thrived (without benefit of capitals or punctuation)
in a newspaper office of the 1920s, amusing the world
with their philosophy. warty bliggens was a frog who
considered himself center of the universe, "the earth exist-
ing to grow toadstools for him to sit under." warty won-
dered merely what the universe had done to deserve him.
archy said if he were a human being he wouldn't laugh

too complacently at warty bliggens "for similar absurdities have often been lodged in the crinkles of the human cerebrum." It's handy, particularly when you feel yourself made important by pain, to remember warty.

OCTOBER 21

Little minds are wounded by little things. Great minds see all and are not even hurt.   Old Proverb

OCTOBER 22

It's a quiet, blessed month. I used to love the early spring the best, but now I'm in the fall of life and the fall of the year agrees with my advancing years. Everything is calm and mellow and ripe. . . . The walnut trees have faded and are dropping their fruit. Persimmons are ripe and possum too. The little boys are pulling their pop corn and digging their goobers and gathering chestnuts and haws and May pops. The nights are getting long and a little fire takes off the evening chill and cheers the family hearth-stone. Now is the time to read and write and have some old-time music.   Bill Arp

OCTOBER 23

'Brer Rabbit was obleeged to climb a tree.'

Joel Chandler Harris

One of the best beloved of the Uncle Remus stories is the one about the poor beleaguered rabbit, one of Joel Chandler Harris' favorite heroes. So hard pressed was Brer Rabbit by his arch foe Brer Fox that he climbed a tree.

"'But, Uncle Remus,' said the little boy, 'a rabbit can't climb a tree.'

"'Don't you mind that, honey,' said Uncle Remus. 'Brer Fox pressed this rabbit so hard he was 'bleeged to climb a tree!'"

Many of us would never accomplish anything if we weren't, like Brer Rabbit, "'bleeged" to.

OCTOBER 24

Speak hopefully for 24 hours.   Norman Vincent Peale

It's not an easy task, but Dr. Peale vows that it will change your outlook and be a power for good in your life. To that admonition he adds these: 1. Continue the practice of speaking hopefully for one week and then be realistic for a day or two. 2. Underscore every sentence about faith in the four gospels of the New Testament. 3. Commit the underscored to memory. 4. Cultivate your positive friends. 5. Avoid argument. Counter negative attitudes with positive, optimistic opinion. 6. Pray.

OCTOBER 25

Hide your offended heart. Keep your valued friend.
Chinese Proverb

OCTOBER 26

He giveth power to the faint; and to them that have no might he increaseth strength. . . . They that wait upon the Lord shall renew their strength; they shall mount up with wings as eagles; they shall run, and not be weary; and they shall walk and not faint.   Isaiah 40:29, 31

OCTOBER 27

Let all bitterness, and wrath, and anger, and clamour, and evil speaking, be put away from you.

Ephesians 4:31

OCTOBER 28

Money like manure does no good till it is spread.

Old Proverb

OCTOBER 29

Exactness in little duties is a wonderful source of cheerfulness. F. W. Faber (Muv's collection)

OCTOBER 30

It is more dishonourable to distrust a friend than to be deceived by him. Old Proverb

OCTOBER 31

O Thou, who kindly dost provide
For every creature's want!
We bless Thee, God of nature wide,
For all Thy goodness lent:
And if it pleases Thee, heavenly Guide,
But whether granted or denied
Lord bless us with content.

Robert Burns

NOVEMBER 1

Now we are done with the last bundle
Of rye and wheat.
What was green in the fields of spring

And bronze in summer's
Is now meal in the barrel
Or bread to eat.

This was no labor of love
But sweat will sweeten
The bread from the salted brow;
When the snows come
We will give grave thanks for bread, eaten
To the last crumb.

Byron Herbert Reece

NOVEMBER 2

I think now happiness is a thing you practice like music until you have skill in striking the right notes on time. We have no vocation for it. And I had no practice, not a day when I was free from care and one great anxiety—and one must be free to be happy. I know that much about it by having missed it.   Corra Harris

NOVEMBER 3

A home is not a mere transient shelter: its essence lies in its permanence . . . in its quality of representing in all its

*details the personalities of the people who live in it. . . .
It is at once a refuge from the world, a treasure-house, a
castle and the shrine of a whole hierarchy of peculiarly
private and potent gods.* H. L. Mencken

NOVEMBER 4

*Six days shalt thou labour and do all thy work; But the
seventh day is the sabbath of the Lord thy God. In it thou
shalt not do any work . . . the Lord blessed the sabbath
day and hallowed it.* Exodus 20:9–11.

My mother Muv has always eschewed work on Sunday,
except that involved in frying chicken and freezing ice
cream and maybe baking the biscuits. Even in those Sunday dinner essentials she has always done as much preparation ahead as is practical. She believes that Sunday
labor is sinful—not only sinful but evidence of bad man-
agement on Saturday. In spite of my raising, I have
labored mightily on Sunday all my adult life, both profes-
sionally and domestically trying to catch up on the week-
end the housekeeping chores I had no time for all week.
But the more I read of Sabbath observance the more I am
attracted to it. Both the Orthodox Jew, who accepts the
thou-shalt-not-labour commandment literally, and the lib-
eral Jew, who acknowledges its spiritual truth, regard the
Sabbath as holy.

To the traditional Jew, writes Rabbi Philip Bernstein, ordinary weekday activities must be set aside "on the hallowed seventh day"—no cooking, riding, lighting of fires, carrying of objects, including money, no fasting if the sabbath should fall on a fast day, no funerals or mourning. "The Sabbath eve nourishes the beauties, the tendernesses, the poetry and the strengths of the Jewish family life," writes Rabbi Bernstein. "It turns the hearts of the parents to the children and the children to the parents. It inspires memories which bless Jews in adversity and console them in sorrow. It sings its way into their hearts. Even physically it helped to sustain the Jews. For no matter how poorly they lived during the week, on the Sabbath, through their own efforts or communal aid, they ate well. . . . The Sabbath, the Jewish way to healing and strength."

NOVEMBER 5

Heroic and pathetic was the figure of this man, groping in the dark for something he had never seen . . . something he very definitely believed he could bring into being for the great good of his people.   Grant Foreman

Less than a hundred miles from where I live there is a restored Indian village called New Echota—the seat of the Cherokees before they were tragically banished to the

West when gold was discovered on their Georgia lands in the 1830s. Here an illiterate Indian genius named Sequoyah—George Guess in English—isolated and characterized eighty-five phonetic sounds in the Cherokee language, the only man in history to conceive and perfect in its entirety an alphabet or syllabary. Thus the Cherokees became the only North American Indian tribe to have a written language and eventually their own newspaper, the *Cherokee Phoenix,* published at New Echota. Ridiculed by his tribesmen, Sequoyah worked twelve years to perfect his alphabet—toiling, striving patiently alone "with no human being to bear him company," as Foreman wrote, "none to understand or encourage, none with whom he could communicate or ask counsel, unable to read in any language and therefore unable to call to his aid any of the accumulated wisdom and experience of the white man."

NOVEMBER 6

A man ought to be reconciled to what he can't help, that is unless he owes a little passel of money he can't pay and is reminded of it once a month on a postal card . . . Or unless he has got a lot of sickly no account children. I tell Mrs. Arp we ought to be mighty thankful for there's nary one of our ten that's cross-eyed or knock-kneed or pigeon-toed or box-ankled or sway-backed or hump-shouldered or lame or blind or idiotic and the grandchildren are an improvement upon the stock. I don't believe any of

*'em will ever get to the poorhouse or carry a pistol or go
to the legislature. . . .* Bill Arp

NOVEMBER 7

*Sing it away,
Fling it away.
Laugh it away,
Quaff it away;
Let not blear-eyed Sorrow sit
At thy heart-stone: Throttle it!*

*Drive it away,
Shrive it away,
Shout it away;
Rout it away;
Come thou virgin Joy and be
Life and love and light to me.*

Robert Loveman

NOVEMBER 8

*He who fears to venture as far as his heart urges and his
reason permits is a coward.* Old Proverb

NOVEMBER 9

Being good is without virtue unless you have spirit
enough to be bad.   (Muv's collection)

NOVEMBER 10

You don't believe what you don't see? Did you ever see
your backbone? Some men believe they have a backbone,
when it's nothing but a cotton string run up their backs.

Sam Jones

NOVEMBER 11

For three days in late November, he stood alone, feel-
ing the soft white flakes of Time falling out of the infinite
cold steel sky, silently, softly, feathering the roof and
powdering the eaves. He stood, eyes shut. The attic, wal-
lowed in seas of wind in the long sunless days, creaked
every bone and shook down ancient dusts from its beams

*and warped timbers and lathings. It was a mass of sighs
and torments that ached all about him where he stood
sniffing its elegant dry perfumes and feeling of its ancient heritages. . . . Consider an attic. Its very atmosphere is Time. It deals in other years, the cocoons and
chrysalises of another age. All the bureau drawers are little coffins where a thousand yesterdays lie in state. Oh,
the attic's a dark, friendly place, full of Time, and if you
stand in the very center of it, straight and tall, squinting
your eyes, and thinking and thinking, and smelling the
Past, and putting out your hands to feel of Long Ago,
why, it . . .* Ray Bradbury

Ray Bradbury is not only one of the most original and
imaginative writers in the language, he's a kind man.
Once I wanted to give his *A Medicine for Melancholy*,
from which the above was taken, to a friend for
Christmas. The friend, a young writer, admired Mr. Bradbury so much I undertook to get an autograph, explaining
to the author that my friend was trying to write but often
grew very discouraged. Ray Bradbury went to considerable trouble to be sure we got the autograph in time for
Christmas—and I had been running late with the whole
thing, of course. More than that he confessed his own
doubts and despair of twenty years before. A writer, he
pointed out, has only himself to offer the world. "There is
only one of him in the world," he wrote. "And it is the
precious difference, isolated, rarefied, set down, encap-
suled. Good luck. Merry Christmas!"

NOVEMBER 12

Not to be Ministered Unto, but to Minister.
Words on Martha Berry's tombstone

When I was young I used to delight in collecting funny
epitaphs, but as I grow older I find the messages on tomb-
stones are often serious summations of the life of the
dead. Willie Snow Etheridge, a delightfully humorous
writer, once said she likes to travel so much her husband,
Mark, has vowed to put on her tombstone when she dies:
"The Lord called her—and she could go."

One of the best epitaphs I ever read is the one Benjamin Franklin wrote for himself but couldn't persuade
his family to use. It says:

The Body of Benjamin Franklin, Printer,
(Like the Cover of An Old Book, Its Contents Torn
Out and Stript of its Lettering and Gilding)
Lies here, food for worms.
But the work shall not be lost for it will (as he
believed) appear once more in a new and more elegant
edition
Revised and Corrected by
The Author.

NOVEMBER 13

The wise know too well their weaknesses to assume infallibility; and he who knows most knows best how little he knows.   Thomas Jefferson

NOVEMBER 14

How does one practice discipline? Our grandfathers would have been much better equipped to answer this question. Their recommendation was to get up early in the morning, not to indulge in unnecessary luxuries, to work hard. This type of discipline had obvious shortcomings. It was rigid and authoritarian, was centered around the virtues of frugality and saving, and in many ways was hostile to life. But in a reaction to this kind of discipline, there has been an increasing tendency to be suspicious of any discipline, and to make undisciplined, lazy indulgence in the rest of one's life the counterpart and balance for the routinized way of life imposed on us during the eight hours of work. To get up at a regular hour, to devote a regular amount of time during the day to activities such as meditating, reading, listening to music, walking; not to indulge, at least beyond a certain minimum, in escapist activities like mystery stories and movies, not to overeat or overdrink are some obvious and rudimentary rules.   Erich Fromm

NOVEMBER 15

My problem is ME.
                          One Day at a Time in Al-Anon

"Trying to analyze why another person persists in destructive behavior cannot help me out of my own difficulties," says this little book. "I can overcome them only by turning my thoughts inward, to face my own mistakes and to learn how to improve myself. The alcoholic is not my problem. My problem is me."

NOVEMBER 16

Four Fine Things: Goodness of Heart, Freedom of Spirit, Gaiety of Temper and Friendliness of Disposition.
                          Helen and Horace Johnson

NOVEMBER 17

A foolish consistency is the hobgoblin of little minds.
                                        Ralph Waldo Emerson

To a woman, consistency is one of those qualities you value in your friends but somehow can't achieve in yourself. Happily, Mr. Emerson doesn't think it's worth worrying about. "The other terror that scares us . . . ," he wrote, "is our consistency. . . . With consistency a great soul has simply nothing to do. . . . Speak what you think now . . . and tomorrow speak what tomorrow thinks. . . . There will be an agreement in whatever variety of actions, so they be each honest and natural in their hour. . . ."

NOVEMBER 18

You work that you may keep pace with the earth and the soul of the earth. For to be idle is to become a stranger unto the seasons, and to step out of life's procession, that marches in majesty and proud submission towards the infinite. When you work you are a flute through whose heart the whispering of the hours turns to music.

*Which of you would be a reed, dumb and silent, when all
else sings together in unison?*   Kahlil Gibran

The Syrian author of *The Prophet* became a coffee-table
poet a few years ago—a sort of display item—and I am
sorry because he represented to me something wonder-
fully grown-up and esoteric for years. He helped to
unlock a stubborn door in my mind when I was a high
school freshman. I had failed first-year Latin and was taking it again with no interest or hope whatever. To escape
the thought of it, I used to spend my study hours in the
library reading poetry. One day I found my former Latin
teacher, Miss Grey Gibson, working as assistant librarian.
Instead of reprimanding me for time-wasting, she
browsed through the poetry shelves with me, suggesting
things. One day she brought from home her own copy of
The Prophet to lend me. It was an honor to borrow a
teacher's personal book—and such a sophisticated book,
too, with naked pictures even. I was overwhelmed and
ripe for it when Miss Gibson remarked casually that she
was surprised I hadn't liked Latin because it is "such a
romantic language." Romantic? I never heard of such a
thing. She talked a little more about its being a language
important to poets and all good writers and, unbelievably,
something to enjoy rather than suffer over. I left with *The
Prophet* under my arm and a whole new approach toward
Latin in my mind. It wasn't easy, but I passed it and was
even sorry I couldn't take more.

NOVEMBER 19

So long as your heart receives messages of beauty, cheer, courage, grandeur and power from the earth, from man and from the Infinite, so long you are young.

Samuel Ullman (Muv's collection)

NOVEMBER 20

It is a pity that things weren't arranged so that an empty head, like an empty stomach, would not let us rest until we put something in it.   Red Gray

NOVEMBER 21

I want the political parties of this country to crawl up out of the mud and wash themselves from head to foot and put on clean clothes before I have anything to do with them.   Sam Jones 1900

NOVEMBER 22

*It's comin' 'long, Thanksgivin', with all its love
and light,
It's dinner in the daytime, it's melodies at night.
The turkey's fat and juicey, the table silver's set,
And we're feelin' mighty happy that we're all alivin'
yet!*

Frank L. Stanton

Early in this century Frank L. Stanton's name was known throughout the world. He was a daily columnist for the Atlanta *Constitution,* so popular and so widely read that he stopped a suicide in Chicago and a hanging in Texas just with his verses. He is best known for two songs, "Mighty Lak a Rose" and "Just a-Wearying for You." Not a great many years ago I did a story on the sale of his old home by his daughter, Marcelle Stanton Megahee. After the story appeared in the paper, Mrs. Megahee decided to give me some reminder of the family and the old house. She said she was sending me "a little something" and I anticipated maybe an ashtray or a flower pot. What came was a Victorian love seat upholstered in red velvet—and so splendid I wrung my hands in distress over preserving it in a houseful of dogs and children. "That's all right," my mother Muv comforted me, "everybody needs something that is too fine for them."

NOVEMBER 23

When ye have gathered in the fruit of the land, ye shall keep a feast unto the Lord . . . and ye shall rejoice before the Lord your God seven days.   Leviticus 23:39–40

Thanksgiving, contrary to what we teach our children, is not a peculiarly American festival which started in 1621 with Governor Bradford and the Pilgrim Fathers. It goes back to the Canaanites from whom the children of Israel took many of their customs. Hebrews have longed celebrated it with their Feast of Tabernacles. Even the Romans gave thanks—to their harvest deity Ceres. Harvest Home was an ancient observance in England.

As it says in the book of Judges (9:27): "And they went out into the field and gathered their vineyards and trod the grapes and held festival and went into the house of their god and did eat and drink. . . ."

NOVEMBER 24

"Tain't much, but it's the best we got, and you're sure welcome."   Quoted by Marjorie Kinnan Rawlings

The welcome is the thing, says Mrs. Rawlings, and it's especially to be remembered at Thanksgiving. "Two elements enter into successful and happy gatherings at table," she writes. "The food, whether simple or elaborate, must be carefully prepared; willingly prepared; imaginatively prepared. And the guests—friends, family or strangers—must be conscious of their welcome. Formal dinners of ill-assorted folk invited for the sole purpose of repaying social obligations are an abomination. The breaking of bread together, the sharing of salt, is too ancient a symbol of friendliness to be profaned. At the moment of dining, the assembled group stands for a little while as a safe unit, under a safe roof, against the perils and enmities of the world. The group will break up and scatter, later. For this short time, let them eat, drink and be merry."

NOVEMBER 25

Take a bucket and fill it with water,
Put your hand in it, up to the wrist,
Pull it out, and the hole that's remaining,
Is a measure of how you'll be missed.

Anonymous

My father didn't know this poem but I wish he had. He valued humility and he said so often that nobody is indispensable. The poem says of the hand-in-the-bucket ploy:
The moral in this quaint example
Is do just the best that you can,
Be proud of yourself, but remember,
There is no indispensable man.

NOVEMBER 26

I believe that the rendering of useful service is the common duty of mankind and that only in the purifying fire of sacrifice is the dross of selfishness consumed and the greatness of the human soul set free.

John D. Rockefeller, Jr.

NOVEMBER 27

Nobody, but nobody, drinks Canadian Club on Skid Row.   Wilson A. Barkman

In New York, where Wilson Barkman gathered most of his experience for his autobiographical *Winos, Dine-o's and Ding-Bats*, the poor drunk's drink is called Sneaky Pete or Sweet Lucy and consists of a cheap fortified wine which costs about sixty cents a fifth. In Atlanta there's a highly alcoholic shaving lotion called "Miss Peach," which serves when nothing else is available. For years Harold Martin and I had a coterie of down-on-their-luck, down-at-the-heels alcoholics who hit us regularly for fifty cents to buy "Miss Peach." Once when one of them came to call I told him that I had decided to stop giving him these small handouts but to spend such piddling funds as I had to dispense on milk for children. He bowed deeply. He really was a courtly fellow in a soiled, moth-eaten way. He said he certainly understood and he would not bother me again but there was a point he thought I had overlooked. The world is full of people dispensing milk to children but did I know of anybody else who would give a drunk with a burning thirst surcease?

"You can always try Antabuse," I said somewhat spitefully. He shuddered delicately and departed—to stay away about five years.

He came back recently, looking so spruce and smart, so sober, I almost didn't recognize him. He had joined Alcoholics Anonymous and been sober about a year. He had a job, a neat little apartment, and a cat named Serenity for the A.A.'s prayer. He came by because he thought his good news would cheer me up, he said, and besides he wanted me to put the word in the paper that the A.A.'s "greater power" step wasn't so bad. He'd worried about being asked to believe in and rely on God, he said. ("Too much hellfire and damnation talk in my childhood!") But he found it was up to him what he believed and he found he wanted to.

"When you get low enough to say, 'God help me,' and mean it, you're ready to begin," he said.

NOVEMBER 28

I have not herd the result of my election from all the countys I expict I am beaton I have one Consolation I would rather be beaton and be a man than to be elected and be a little puppy dog.   David Crockett

NOVEMBER 29

The conditions of virtue are independent of outer things. It makes little difference what you are, prince or peasant, for all are imperfect. A true and honest life alone counts.   Indian Philosophy

NOVEMBER 30

Keep us, oh God, from smallness. Let us be large in thought, in word and in deed. Let us have done with complaint and leave off self-seeking. May we put away all pretense and meet each other with pity and without prejudice. May we never be hasty in Judgment of others. Make us always generous. Let us take time to be calm and gentle. Teach us to put into action our better impulses and to walk unafraid. Grant that we may realize that the little things of life are those which create our differences and that in the big things of life, we are as one under God. And, O Lord, let us never forget to be kind. Amen.

Mary Queen of Scots before she
went to her execution

DECEMBER 1

What silly heavens in the skies
The prating prophets plan!
Some unimagined, vast surprise
Shall greet the soul of man!

Robert Loveman

DECEMBER 2

What is success and in what does it consist? In heaping
up accumulations of money and property by over-reach-
ing the public and crushing competition? In greasing the
axles of progress with the blood of the poor and the igno-
rant? In adding to the doubts and thereby increasing the
misery of the people of the nations of the earth? Or does
it consist in living a clean and wholesome life, in making
the troubles of your neighbors your own, in avoiding envy
and all forms of covetousness and in thanking Heaven for
what you have, however small a portion that may be?
There can be no form of real success that does not bring
some sort of aid and comfort to humanity, that does not

*make people a little happier, a little more contented than
they were before, that does not uplift in some sort the soul
which the German professor does not find in his cadavers
and that does not bring joy and content from the shallow
well of life.*   Joel Chandler Harris

Such solemn exposition on human hopes and aspirations
was not unusual for Joel Chandler Harris. He wrote editorials for the Atlanta *Constitution* daily and also published
his own *Uncle Remus Magazine,* dedicated to what he
considered most important—"neighbor-knowing." But he
was best known and loved for his stories for children.
They drew famous people from all over the world to him.
When President Theodore Roosevelt and his wife visited
Atlanta they wrote ahead and asked if they might meet
the man whose stories they read to their children. Although he was very modest and almost pathologically shy,
Mr. Harris could not turn them down. They became such
friends that he later went to visit them in the White
House and wrote one of his dialect stories about it, attributing the visit to a character he called Mr. Billy Sanders.

"Thar's one thing about the White House that'll astonish you ef you ever git thar while Teddy is on hand.
It's a home; it'll come over you like a sweet dream the
minnit you git in the door and you'll wonder how they
sweep out all the politics and keep the place clean an'
wholesome."

When Mr. Harris died in 1908, Grantland Rice wrote,

There's a shadow on the cotton patch,
The blue has left the sky.
And his colleague on the *Constitution,* Frank L. Stanton wrote:
He dreamed the dreams of Childhood, giving
Joy to the wide world's end;
For in the man the child was living
And little children called him friend.

DECEMBER 3

Right effort cannot be isolated from right thinking.
Radhakrishnan

DECEMBER 4

Often I think it would be fine if the French poodle could take over the world, because they've certainly been more intelligent in the last few years than the human being, and they have great charm, grace, humor and intelligence. James Thurber

Thurber couldn't have known my mother Muv's dog, Jackie, who is a marvel to us all. How could he write so knowledgeably about the qualities of her kind without knowing her? Jackie's arrival a few years ago has changed the "I" of Muv's life to "We." The frisky little puppy adapted herself completely to the ways of an elderly woman. She gets up when Muv does, goes to bed when Muv does, and even comes in from the yard and curls up at the foot of Muv's bed when it's afternoon nap time. She is somebody to talk to, somebody to cook for, and somebody to come home to—a patient little waiter-by-the-gate when Muv goes to the store or to church, an interested and inquisitive companion when there's yardwork to be done, and she likes the Lawrence Welk show.

DECEMBER 5

There are people who never really enjoy life and never really suffer. Life goes on for them like music played con sordino, *with a mute, without the extreme tone colors. They don't know the ability of enjoyment; they haven't really lived.*   Joseph Wechsberg

DECEMBER 6

I am young and strong and I am living a great adventure; I am still in the midst of it and can't grumble the whole day long. I have been given a lot, a happy nature, a great deal of cheerfulness and strength. Every day I feel that I am developing inwardly, that the liberation is drawing nearer and how beautiful nature is, how good the people are about me, how interesting this adventure is! Why then should I be in despair? Anne Frank

The Diary of Anne Frank should be required reading for those of us who are given to restlessness, discontent, anxiety and depression. A child, a fourteen-year-old girl, held prisoner, unable to open a window or touch the earth, fearful of every knock on the door, sickened by the knowledge that her friends had been hauled off to die, could still regard living as "a great adventure," still hope for liberation and still ask, "Why then should I be in despair?"

DECEMBER 7

*Humility is the most difficult of all virtues to achieve;
nothing dies harder than the desire to think well of one-
self.*   T. S. Eliot

DECEMBER 8

*The Bible is a storehouse of individual spiritual revela-
tion and release. It appeals to every class, taste and mood.
It depicts king and pauper; saint and sinner. It is tragic
and humorous. It is violent and gentle. It is proud and
meek. It is beseeching and triumphant . . . If it means
nothing to you at first, keep at it and if you do, almost
suddenly you will come to see and understand many
things which in the duration of a lifetime could never
have been satisfactorily explained to you by someone else.*
                                     Virginia Cary Hudson

DECEMBER 9

I have an instinctive fear of the psychological effect of surveys. A fellow can get in the habit of feeling his pulse too frequently. . . . The signers of the Declaration of Independence did not take a poll before they acted. They were aware of the great opposition and said so plainly, by noting that they were risking their fortunes, their honor and their lives by doing so. Jefferson, Jackson, Wilson and others all led—they did not act like weather vanes. The status-quo mentality is not wisdom.   Ralph McGill

Ralph McGill, famous editor of the Atlanta *Constitution* and my boss for many years, scolded and shamed, coaxed and persuaded our part of the world toward integration long before some areas of the South had even considered it. As Harold Martin wrote of him in his fine biography, *Ralph McGill, Reporter,* he was a "tremendously warm-hearted, loving, angry, sometimes wrong-headed, stubborn and exasperating man—an Old Testament prophet touched with the grace of tenderness and humor." But he did not consider himself a top-flight crusader. He wrote:

> *"In matters controversial*
> *My perception's very fine,*
> *I always see both sides of things—*
> *The one that's wrong and mine."*

And he added, "I am not a good crusader. I call my shots. And I aim where I think a shot is needed. And I recall often the old motto, Lord give me this day my daily idea and forgive me the one I had yesterday."

DECEMBER 10

A famous teacher once told his students that everyone should have two pockets so that, according to his needs, he could reach into the one or the other. In his right pocket is to be a slip of paper with the words, "For my sake was the world created," and in his left pocket one with the words, "I am dust and ashes." There is a time for each.   Rabbi Samuel H. Dresner

DECEMBER 11

For many years, I had an idea that nature had for man an active sympathy; but now I have changed my opinion. There seems really a superb indifference about nature. It is what lies behind nature that really has sympathy. The rose does not of itself bloom for us; but God has made it bloom for us. Surely this beauty is not a random affair; it is too authentically a sign and symbol of love.
                                        Archibald Rutledge

DECEMBER 12

Of course each of us thinks his neighbor should be more dedicated. Our own passion for dedication is contaminated by selfishness, laziness and inconstancy but our ardor for the other fellow's dedication is pure and undefiled. . . . Artemus Ward said, "I have already given two cousins to the war and I stand ready to sacrifice my wife's brother. . . ." John W. Gardner

DECEMBER 13

Some old-fashioned things are good yet. I have even got respect for my rheumatism for it has stuck by me like a friend for a long time and it is nearly the only disease that has not changed its name and its pain since I was a boy. Bill Arp

DECEMBER 14

As I have grown older I am more and more convinced that I have not grown up, that my powers have not come

to me, not my real wisdom to do and achieve the right thoughts. I lack some dear grace. . . . There is a curriculum in living in which I have not studied. This may be happiness. I want to know it; I should feel better prepared for immortality. I do not wish to arrive fagged at last and a bit slipshod in the spirit, as if I had a hard time all my mortal life. It is not complimentary to God.

Corra Harris

DECEMBER 15

Four things which are not in thy treasury,
I lay before thee, Lord, with this petition:
My nothingness, my wants,
My sins and my contrition.

Robert Southey

DECEMBER 16

"The human heart is allus the same. Sorrow strikes the same all over. Hit makes a different kind o' mark in different places. Jest be a leetle mite easy on t'other feller."   Penny Baxter in *The Yearling*

DECEMBER 17

Yours the message cheering
That the time is nearing
Which will see
All men free,
Tyrants disappearing.

"Mo'oz Tzur"—Hebrew Hymn

While Gentiles are getting ready for Christmas, Jews stage a December (or late November) celebration nearly as long—the eight days of Chanukah, commemorating the Jewish nation's successful revolt against the decree of King Antiochus IV in the year 168 B.C. that they worship an idol he set up in the Temple of Jerusalem. The Jews refused, drove the Syrians out, and rededicated the Temple. At that time they burned a cruse of oil which lasted eight days. Nowadays they light a series of candles during the eight days of celebration, one on the first night, two on the second, and so on. A renowned rabbi once explained the difference between the observance of Purim, a gala carnival, and the more solemn Chanukah. "On Purim we were saved from the attempt to destroy the body of the Jew; but on Chanukah we were rescued from the decree that would have destroyed our soul."

DECEMBER 18

*If negative goodness was religion, then one of those
lamp posts out there would be the best Christian in town;
it never cursed, nor swore; nor drank a drop since it was
made; it never did anything wrong.*   Sam Jones

DECEMBER 19

An event occurred in Palestine . . .
                                Bishop Warren Akin Candler

In the 1920s it was the fashion for people to point out that
much of the Christmas celebration was derived from
pagan goings on and December 25 probably wasn't the
date of Jesus' birth anyhow. Bishop Candler had small patience with such pickiness. "It is a matter of small moment whether men have, or have not, fixed upon the correct date for the annual celebration of the birth of our
Lord," he said. "It remains too clear for doubt that some
1900 years ago an event occurred in Palestine which has
been more influential for good among men than all the
efforts of the sages and statements of the ages. The brief

life, with a manger cradle at one end and a borrowed
tomb at the other, was spent in poverty deeper than that
of the birds of the air and the foxes of the forest. And yet
from it has sprung all of the riches, both material and im-
material, found in what we call Christian civilization. The
outcome of that life is the miracle of history."

DECEMBER 20

*Grandpa Parris used to say there was nothing like a
water-soaked hickory stump for a yule log.*   John Parris

At this season of the year, the loveliest and most reverent
in the calendar, we are so caught up in rush and excitement we sometimes leave the matter of the Yule log alone
and settle for burning whatever is on the woodpile. This is
a mistake, of course, because according to legend, no one
works while the Yule log burns. Writing of old days in the
North Carolina mountains, John Parris said it was the cus-
tom to search out the hickory stumps on the Little Savan-
nah River and pick the biggest you could fit into your
hearth. From the time the log was lighted on Christmas
Eve until it settled into ashes everybody just folded their
hands and rested. A log that burned two or three days
was a great boon to those who had worn themselves out in
getting ready for Christmas.

DECEMBER 21

Some say that ever 'gainst that season comes
Wherein our Saviour's birth is celebrated,
The bird of dawning singeth all night long:
And then, they say, no spirit dare stir abroad;
The nights are wholesome; then no planets strike,
No fairy takes, nor witch hath power to charm,
So hallow'd and so gracious is the time.

Marcellus in *Hamlet*

It has been my ambition all my life to stay up on Christmas Eve to see if the animals talked, as they are supposed to at the hour of the Baby's birth. I've never made it, being either too sleepy or too busy trying to put toys together with no more suitable tools than nail files and beer can openers. But I believe the legend that at the moment of the Saviour's birth there was a great calm on the earth with all nature pausing in reverent adoration and then the animals began to talk. What did they say? According to the old tales, they spoke in Latin. The cook crowed *"Christus natus est"* (Christ is born); the raven asked, *"Quando?"* (When?); the crow answered, *"Hac nocte* (This night). The ox put in *"Ubi?"* (Where?) and the lamb said, "Bethlehem."

DECEMBER 22

Whoso shall receive one such little child in my name receiveth me.   Matthew 18:5

All of us are thinking about children at this season and I think it is interesting that Matthew, alone among the four evangelists, tells of the Wise Men and the gifts to the Baby Jesus. It is his message that "When we minister to little children, we minister unto Him."

DECEMBER 23

Of all the trees in the wood the holly bears the crown.
                                    English Song

The legend that the holly tree, which abounds in southern woods and is used in so much of our Christmas decorations, was also the tree used for the crucifixion brings a sad note to Christmas. Its thorns are sharp, its bark as bitter as gall, its berries as red as blood, the song reminds us. Earl W. Count says "The music of the Natal morn has its dark strain. . . . It has always been there," he writes. "The common folk of the Middle Ages, and those who are their descendants in the simple wisdom sprung from their lives, have never shrunk from the note of sadness, of coming tragedy for which this birthday is a preparation. Sometimes it sounds in their carols; yet we hear no discord; only a sweet and finer and deeper music."

DECEMBER 24

If I but had a little coat,
A coat to fit a no-year-old
I'd button it close about His throat
To cover Him from the cold,
    The cold,
To cover Him from the cold.

                • • •

If my heart were a shining coin,
A silver coin or a coin of gold
Out of my side I'd it purloin
And give it to Him to hold,
    To Hold,
And give it to Him to hold.

                                Byron Herbert Reece

This is the night we always reread the Christmas ballads of the lanky mountain poet Byron Reece, who lived a short life and is lovingly remembered by so many of us. When Mr. McGill died and the things in his office were to be removed to Emory University library for saving in its special collections department, Mrs. McGill asked those of us who had known and loved him to pick something from his bookshelves to keep. I picked a book which Bryon autographed to him in 1952 and later Mrs. McGill sent me a picture to go with it. It showed the mountain farmer and his parents by the fireplace in their old house. It had been taken on one of the many occasions when Mr. McGill and Harold Martin looked in on Byron, worried about his health (he had tuberculosis), his financial state, and his loneliness. They always came away richer for having sat and visited awhile with the young man who thought and talked in the lyrical ballad style of the sixteenth and seventeenth centuries.

I have always considered my brief friendship with him one of the great gifts in my life—especially at Christmas.

DECEMBER 25

My soul doth magnify the Lord,
And my spirit hath rejoiced in God my Saviour.
For he hath regarded the low estate of his handmaiden;
For, behold, from henceforth all generations shall
call me blessed.
For he that is mighty hath done to me great things;
and holy is his name.

And his mercy is on them that fear him from
generation to generation.
He hath shewed strength with his arm; he hath
scattered the proud in the imagination of
their hearts.
He hath put down the mighty from their seats, and
exalted them of low degree.
He hath filled the hungry with good things; and the
rich he hath sent empty away.
He hath holpen his servant Israel in remembrance
of his mercy.

Luke 1:46–54

DECEMBER 26

Well, we have had our Christmas and our Christmas
turkey and got well of it.   Bill Arp

The old philosopher puts it so simply and naturally that
we don't feel compelled to try to sustain the mood of
Christmas after the day is gone. We are free to relax and
to think of other things.

DECEMBER 27

So I went to school. And I learned a lot of stuff. If they make you go where learning is flying around, some of it is bound to light on you. Leroy (Satchel) Paige

DECEMBER 28

Like a ten-ton cake the world is more than anyone can eat at one sitting. Select a piece of it, then, and enjoy the party. Samuel M. Silver

DECEMBER 29

There is a day of sunny rest
For every dark and troubled night;
And grief may hide an evening guest
But joy shall come with early light.

William Cullen Bryant

DECEMBER 30

The cry of the Old Year to the New Year is: Hold fast to
the good things and make them better as fast as you can.
                              Bishop Warren Akin Candler

DECEMBER 31

I said to a man who stood at the gate of the year: "Give
me a light that I may tread safely into the unknown." And
he replied, "Go out into the darkness and put your hand
into the hand of God. That shall be better than a light
and safer than a known way."

Quoted by King George VI to
close his Christmas address to the
British people in 1939